A GREAT WEEKEND IN

FLORENCE

A GREAT WEEKEND IN
FLORENCE

When you first start to explore Florence, you may get the impression that the city that invented the Renaissance is still firmly in the grip of its illustrious past. But like so many famous visitors before you, you'll soon discover that behind the many palaces, churches and museums full of masterpieces lies a Florence that is far from being as austere and haughty as is sometimes said. So put on your walking shoes and set out to discover the city of a thousand secrets.

Your first surprise will come when, in spite of all the effort you put into learning Italian, you don't understand a word the hotel receptionist is saying. What you have to remember is that the Florentines, who imposed the language of Dante on the rest of Italy, pronounce it differently from other Italians, aspirating the consonants, in particular 'c', so they say 'hoha-hola' rather than 'coca-cola'. The second thing you need to be prepared for is that the Florentines, who never miss an opportunity to criticise their own city, will be far from pleased if you agree with them. Of course Florence *is* invaded by tourists for five months of the year, and of course you too wish the marble façades weren't being eaten away by pollution and that traffic wasn't allowed around the Duomo, only it's better not to say so!

Before you do anything else, take to the heights and gaze down on Florence and see it in the setting of the blue-tinged mountains. Alternatively, walk along the banks of the Arno early in the morning, when it barely disturbed by passing rowers and before the city is

given over to hordes of tourists. Then, reassured by its timeless beauty, you can choose your itinerary according to the weather and the monuments and museums you really want to see. You'll find plenty to distract you though – glimpses of faces straight out of paintings by Botticelli or Ghirlandaio, an exhibition that allows you to visit a palace generally closed to the public, an impromptu concert

in a city square, an ice cream you simply can't resist or a tempting shop window. In fact, almost everywhere you turn, you will see something that catches your eye.

As Michelangelo said, 'Those who don't like greenery shouldn't come here in May.' May really is the loveliest month of the year in Florence, with beds of irises carpeting the Piazzale Michelangelo, woody scents wafting from the gardens hidden behind the palaces and the clear blue skies. It's also the month when one of the oldest European music festivals, the *Maggio Musicale*, takes place, though in the city that invented opera, music lovers will find something to occupy their evenings throughout the year.

Despite its reputation as a sleeping beauty, Florence is still very much alive. It's a great financial centre, which is hardly surprising for a city whose power was originally built on trade, and it is also renowned for crafts and men's fashion, two important activities presented at shows at the Fortezza da Basso in late April and January.

If you cross the Arno, you'll discover another side to Florence, not the city of the guide books but the Florence of small craftsmen – gilders, framers, bronze workers, cobblers, bookbinders, weavers and glass cutters – all working in *botteghe* where the same tasks have been carried out since the Middle Ages and where time stands still, since all that counts is fine work. This is where you'll meet the true Florentines, a cultivated courteous, passionate and rational people.

After all these pleasures of the mind, it will be time to sit down at a table in a little trattoria to be served good local fare washed down with delicious chianti. Afterwards you can join in the Italian custom of the *passeggiata* and take a long, well-deserved break on a lively café terrace.

One last word of advice – bring only the bare minimum of luggage since you'll find plenty to tempt you here – soft gloves, smart shoes, leather-bound notebooks, elegant suits, designer pullovers, sophisticated bags, sumptuous silks, fragrant pots-pourris, embroidered tablecloths, dreamy underwear, stylish lamps and glazed terracotta, not to mention all the good things to eat that you'll want to take back with you in order to recapture the delicious flavours of the weekend. But really, there's only one thing for it – if you can't take everything home with you, you'll just have to come back again.

How to get to Florence

Florence is beautiful in every season – in the cold light of winter, emerging from the mists of summer or decked in its spring hues, when the city is blue with the irises that are its emblem. If you want to enjoy it to the full, avoid school holidays and rainy months. Reserve concert seats and a room in a charming hotel on the banks of the Arno before you come, pack a comfortable pair of walking shoes – Florence is a place to be explored on foot – and use mosquito repellent from May onwards. If you do all this, you'll be ready to explore one of the loveliest cities in Italy.

THE CLIMATE

Though it can be scorching hot in summer (from 28°C/82°F to 35°C/95°F), you can't always rely on fine weather in Florence. Autumn is the wettest time of year, there are frequent showers in spring and the winters are very severe (from 0°C/32°F to -10°C/14°F). The most pleasant months are May, June and September, but this is also when the tourists arrive in droves, especially during the *Maggio Musicale* festival beginning in the third week of April. Avoid the school holidays if you can, especially over Easter. In August, the sweltering city is deserted by its inhabitants, who go to the seaside for a break from the heat. If you're mainly interested in culture, this is a good time to come and spend a weekend in Florence as the hotels have special offers. On the other hand, don't expect to be able to go on a shopping spree or visit the craft workshops since most businesses are closed during August.

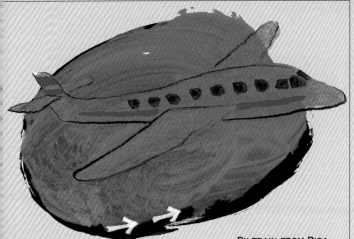

HOW TO GET THERE

BY PLANE

If you're only going for a short break, it's best to go by plane.

Only one airline operates direct flights from the UK, London Gatwick, to Florence Amerigo Vespucci airport. **Meridiana** is at 15 Charles Street, London SW1
☎ 020 7839 2222
🅕 020 7839 3700.

Otherwise, **British Airways** ☎ 020 7434 4700 or **Alitalia** ☎ 020 7486 8432 fly to Pisa, and from there you can take a train on to Florence from the main station.

None of the international airlines from New Zealand, Australia, the US or Canada fly into Florence. However, there are onward connections from Amsterdam with Meridiana, Brussels with Sabena, Frankfurt with Lufthansa, Paris with Meridiana or Air France and Vienna with Tyrolean.

Outside the UK, Italian Government Travel Offices have useful information:

630 5th Avenue
New York, NY
☎ 212 245 4822
🅕 212 586 9249

550, 12400 Wiltshire Bvd
Los Angeles, Ca
☎ 310 820 1898
🅕 310 820 6357

1914, 1 Place Ville-Marie
Montreal, Canada
☎ 514 866 7668
🅕 514 866 7667
(brochure line)
🅕 514 392 1429

c/o Italian Chamber of Commerce and Industry
Level 26, 44 Market St, Sydney
☎ 292 621666
🅕 292 625745

The most comprehensive web site for information about Florence is www.mega.it. This lists information about all the sites, hotels, restaurants, festivals and other events. Some have on-line booking options.

BY TRAIN FROM PISA

The train journey from Pisa airport to Florence is simple. There's one train an hour from the station at the Galileo Galilei airport, and the journey, costing around L12,000, takes an hour. You arrive at the main station in the middle of Florence.

INCLUSIVE BREAKS

Many tour operators offer two- and three-day weekend breaks that include air travel and accommodation in various categories of hotel. For the best rates, you have to spend Saturday night in Florence. The main attraction of these breaks is that they give you the chance to stay at a luxury hotel (Helvetia & Bristol, Villa Medici, Grand Hotel, Regency, Baglioni, Excelsior or Villa Cora) for a very reasonable price. You also benefit from the rates negotiated by tour operators and travel more cheaply while avoiding the bother of booking. An extensive list of tour operators

who organise weekend breaks can be obtained from the Italian State Tourist Office, whose address and telephone/ fax numbers can be found in the yellow box on p. 8. Alternatively, you could compare prices from:

Bridge Travel Services
55-59 High Rd, Broxbourne, Herts EN10 7DT
☎ 01992 456 600
🅵 01992 456 609 or e-mail cities@bridge-travel.co.uk.

Citalia
Marco Polo House, 3-5 Lansdowne Rd, Croydon CR9 1LL
☎ 020 8686 5533
🅵 020 8681 0712 or e-mail ciao@citalia.co.uk

Lupus Travel Ltd
Triumph House, 189 Regent St., London W1R 7WD
☎ 020 7306 3000
🅵 020 7287 2142.

Some two and three-star hotels are unappealing 'tourist factories' that accommodate groups all year round. For a selection of smaller, often family-run hotels, contact:

HPS Hotel Reservations
Archgate, 823-825 High Rd, North Finchley, London N12 8UB
☎ 020 8446 0126
🅵 020 8446 0196 or e-mail res@hotel-reserve.com.

Accommodation Line Ltd
1/46 Maddox Street, London W1R 9PB
☎ 020 7409 1343
🅵 020 7409 2606.

ARRIVING BY PLANE

The little Amerigo Vespucci airport is 6km/4 miles north-west of Florence. The bus company **Sita** runs buses to the railway station from 8am to 8pm, with departures approximately every hour. The journey costs L6,000 and you can buy a ticket from ticket machines or on the bus. If you haven't got too much to carry, walk 150m/yds to the Ataf bus stop and catch an orange 62 bus. This runs from 6.30am to 11.30pm, departing every twenty minutes on weekdays and every thirty-five minutes on Saturdays and holidays. You can buy a ticket for L3,000 from the driver (instead of L1,500 from the bar of the departure hall). Either way, it'll take you twenty minutes to get to Santa Maria Novella station, and from there you'll have a choice of taxi or small bus (lines A, B and D) to take you to your hotel. You can also get a taxi from the airport to the door of your hotel for L30,000-35,000.

HIRING A CAR

It's always cheaper to hire a car from abroad, and you can usually do this through your travel agent. Alternatively, contact one of the international car hire companies to book your car. In Florence, there are car hire companies in the arrivals lounge of the airport and in the city centre. You have to be at least twenty-one to hire a car and have held a full driving licence for at least a year. Ask for the weekend rate.

Europcar
Borgnissanti, 53
☎ 055 236 0072

Herz
Via Finiguerra, 33r
☎ 055 282260

Maggiore
Via Finiguerra, 31r
☎ 055 294578

Italy by Car-Thrifty offers the best weekend rates once you get to Florence:

☎ (091) 60 57 160,
🄵 (091) 60 57 115.
Freefone 1678-68121

Be careful where you park in the city centre – illegally parked cars are quickly towed away.

ENTRY REQUIREMENTS

Citizens of the European Union, including children under 16, must have a valid identity card or passport.

Travellers from the USA, Canada, Australia and New Zealand require a valid passport and are limited to a 90-day stay.

CUSTOMS

Italy is a signatory of the Schengen agreement, so European Union citizens no longer have to pass through customs on arrival in the country. However, if you're travelling by train, your luggage may be searched by French or Italian customs officials, who are constantly on the lookout for illegal substances. Firearms, ammunition, knives, swords, etc., are illegal and cannot be imported. Should you be in any doubt regarding what you can bring into Italy, contact your nearest customs office.

INSURANCE

UK tour operators are obliged by law to offer insurance covering loss of possessions and health and repatriation insurance, but not cancellation and luggage insurance. If you pay for your plane or train ticket with an international credit card, you're automatically entitled to good cover for medical expenses and the cost of repatriation. Otherwise, it's a good idea to take out cover for the cost of repatriation with a reputable insurance company.

HEALTH

If you're on a course of medical treatment, take enough medicines with you when you go because you can't be sure of finding the same ones in Florence. Citizens of European Union countries are entitled to a refund of medical expenses from their Social Security offices on presentation of form E111, which can be obtained from local post offices. In the event of a medical emergency where official assistance is needed, citizens of other countries should contact their nearest consulate or embassy. Representative offices aren't open 24 hours a day, but there'll usually be a recorded message giving a number for use in emergencies. Help will be just a phone call away.

CURRENCY AND CASH

Italy is one of the European Union countries that joined the single currency, and from 2002, the Italian lira will be replaced by the euro (1 euro = L1936.27). In the meantime, all prices are listed in both lire and euros.

It's a good idea to buy lire before you go, partly to get a better exchange rate and partly to give you time to get used to all the zeros. L1,000 is worth around £3, and there are 1,000, 2,000, 5,000, 10,000, 50,000 and 100,000 lire notes, and 50, 100, 200 and 500 lire coins. There are two sizes of 50, 100 and 200 lire coins; the new ones and the old (which are bigger). You may still sometimes be given a telephone token or sweets to make up the change in shops.

PLANNING YOUR WEEKEND

To make the most of your time in Florence, it's a good idea to plan some of your activities in advance.

Italian State Tourist Board
1 Princes St.
London W1R 9AY
☎ 020 7408 1254
🅕 020 7493 6695

Italian Consulate
38 Eaton Place
London SW1
☎ 020 7235 9371

Italian Cultural Institute
39 Belgrave Square
London SW1
☎ 020 7235 1461
🅕 020 7235 4618

Italian Book Shop
8 Cecil Court
London WC2
☎ 020 7240 1634

CIT Italian Tourist agency
Marco Polo House
3-5 Lansdowne Rd
Croydon CR9 1LL
☎ 020 8686 5533
🅕 020 8681 0712
e-mail ciao@citalia.co.uk

British Consulate
Lungarno Corsini, 2
I-50123 Florence
☎ 055 284 133

When changing money before departure, ask for some small-denomination banknotes, as larger notes are hard to change without incurring the wrath (and sometimes refusal) of shopkeepers and clerks.

When you arrive in Florence, you'll find bureaux de change at both the airport

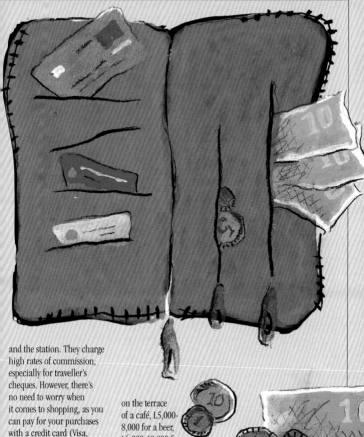

and the station. They charge high rates of commission, especially for traveller's cheques. However, there's no need to worry when it comes to shopping, as you can pay for your purchases with a credit card (Visa, Eurocard, American Express or Diner's Club).

BUDGETING

Florence isn't cheap, but if you've already paid for your hotel, around L500,000 will cover restaurants, outings, museums, shows, etc., once you get there.

Expect to pay L50,000 for a meal with a drink, L5,000-12,000 for a museum ticket, L1,500 for a bus ticket, L1,000-6,000 for a coffee drunk standing at the bar or on the terrace of a café, L5,000-8,000 for a beer, L6,000-10,000 for a cocktail or measure of spirits, L10,000-25,000 to get into a disco, L5,000-40,000 for a theatre or concert ticket and L15,000-25,000 for a taxi ride within the city.

LOCAL TIME

Italy is one hour ahead of Greenwich Mean Time. Summertime starts at the end of March, when clocks are put forward an hour, and wintertime at the end of September, when clocks go back an hour.

VOLTAGE

In Italy, the current is 220 volts. Italian plugs have two or three flat pins and you may need to use an adaptor. It's a good idea to bring one with you or buy one at the airport if you want to be sure of using your electric hairdrier or razor during your stay.

CHIANTI AND OTHER WINES

When we think of Tuscany, we immediately think of Chianti. Yet the well-known bottle wrapped in straw isn't the only wine you see on Florentine tables. There are many other delicious nectars for you to try, including some nice dry white wines. One of these, Vernaccia, was a favourite of Pope Martin IV back in the 13th century.

BARON RICASOLI'S RECIPE

Baron Bettino Ricasoli, a descendant of one of the most illustrious aristocratic families of Tuscany, first made Chianti in 1837. He travelled the length and breadth of France and Germany to study every aspect of wine-growing and imported countless vines. In the end, however, Chianti was born of a combination of three Tuscan vines: *sanglovese* (which essentially provided the bouquet) *canaiolo* (which tempered its roughness) and *malvasia* (which made it lighter and easier to drink). It wasn't until 1932 that the areas of production were fixed, and it

was 1965 before the Ministry of Agriculture designated it D.O.C. (*denominazione di origine controllata*), guaranteeing the production of good-quality wine.

THE CHIANTI RENAISSANCE

Over the last decade, Chianti has returned to its former glory, having acquired a bad reputation following the planting of vines unsuited to the Tuscan soil. However, the introduction of the D.O.C.G. classification in 1984, which was stricter than the earlier D.O.C.,

imposed a reduction in the percentage of white grapes that could be used in the manufacture of red wine. Previously, up to 30% of Chianti was derived from white grapes. This allowed many bad wines to be eliminated. The use of Bordeaux wine bottles in place of the traditional flasks and an effective marketing campaign did the rest. New wines based on a blend of *cabernet sauvignon* and *sangiovese* grapes also made their appearance. Count Contini Bonacassi's example of adding a little *cabernet* to his *carmignano* (D.O.C.) was soon followed by Marquess Antinori, who

demonstrated with *tignanello* that a wine labelled simply *vino di tavola* could become ten times more renowned – and ten times more expensive – than his famous D.O.C.

BRUNELLO DI MONTALCINO, THE JEWEL OF TUSCAN WINE-MAKING

The Montalcino Hills south of Siena are where the most expensive wine in Italy is produced. A wine of exceptional longevity, Brunello di Montalcino, was created in the late 19th century by Ferruccio Biondi-Santi. To obtain a well-structured wine, he selected a clone of the *sangiovese grosso* vine known since the 16th century, whose name (meaning Jupiter's Blood) confirms its age. Very small-scale production and rigorous selection of the hand-picked grapes lead to a very concentrated wine high in tannin, to which it owes the name *brunello*, or 'little brown' wine. Aged for four years in oak tuns and for three in the bottle, it was the first wine to be declared D.O.C.G.

(*denominazione di origine controllata e garantita*– a guaranteed appellation contrôlée). You'll need to be patient to enjoy this wine, because the better the year, the longer you have to wait – twenty years for a good Brunello and fifty for an excellent one. If you're in a hurry, you can fall back on the Rosso di Montalcino, which is lighter and less expensive.

NOBLE WINES

In the south of the Chianti region, where the temperatures are less extreme, a more robust, garnet-coloured wine with the aroma of violets, the D.O.C.G. Vino Nobile di Montepulciano, is produced. Made from local red vines, *prugnolo gentile* (belonging to the *sangiovese* family) and *canaiolo*, it has a D.O.C. equivalent, Rosse di Montepulciano. The potent Vernaccia di San Gimignano, a speciality of the Middle Ages,

is produced in the town of the same name. It was a favourite of the Medicis, as was *vin santo*, a strong but sweet amber-coloured dessert wine that's smooth to drink.

QUICK GUIDE TO CHIANTI

It isn't the quality of the vines that determines the various types of Chianti, but the area of production and nature of the soil. Chianti Classico, which is authenticated by the 'Gallo Nero' (black cockerel) label, a heavier, more complex wine than the other Chiantis, is only produced between Siena and Florence on chalk or clay-schistose soils at an altitude of 150-550m/500-1,800ft. The six Chianti Putto areas produce a lighter wine that is drunk more quickly. Of these, Chianti Rufino and Montalbano have good vintages. Colli Fiorentini and Colli Pisani, which are only produced in small quantities, come close to the best Classicos, while the two latest — Colli Aretini and Colli Senesi — are of more mediocre quality and are used in blends of wine from other parts of Italy.

LEATHER GOODS, A FLORENTINE SPECIALITY

Leatherworking has always been considered a noble art in Florence. The skinners' corporation belonged to the Seven Major Arts. Monks used the finest skins to bind parchments and Gucci's ancestors made saddles for the Florentine aristocracy. Tastes and needs have changed over the centuries but the know-how remains the same and the finest craftsman-made leather goods are still found in Florence.

THE SECRETS OF FINE LEATHER

Tanning is the most important stage in the treatment of skins since it gives the leather its suppleness and prevents it from it rotting. Plants and wooden vats are often used for tanning in Florence for the incomparable finish they give the leather, which also ages better than when tanned with chromium. It can be coloured naturally using aniline powder. Tanning with chromium is the most commonly used method elsewhere because it allows

defects in the leather to be masked when it's polished during the finishing.

SCUOLA DEL CUOIO

After the Second World War, the Franciscans of Santa Croce founded a leather school for young men from poor backgrounds in order to inject new life into a district traditionally associated with the leather trade. Using their long experience of leather-working in the library workshop of the monastery, they taught their pupils the dual trade of bookbinding

and leatherworking. Such is the school's renown that it supplies the White House and the English royal household with luxury office accessories. Under the direction of the Gori family, the workshop still produces high-quality articles worthy of the most famous brand names, but at considerably less cost.

GUCCI

Guccio Gucci, who opened his first shop selling luxury cases and travel articles in the Via

della Vigna Nuova in 1904, used his intertwined initials as a form of trademark. After a short career as an actor in the carefree, frivolous cinema of the inter-war period, his son Rodolfo injected new life into the brand by designing collections of very sophisticated bags. The hallmark of the brand, the Bamboo bag, which first made its appearance in 1947, was based on the shape of a saddle and given a bamboo handle and clasp. It still looks good today.

della Signoria, was the first to make leather desk accessories with designs in gold leaf, a fine craft that has developed considerably over the last few years, always in response to foreign demand.

HAND STITCHED

Don't rely on the 'hand stitched' label often attached to leather goods as a guarantee of quality. All such articles are actually machine stitched by specialist workers. The quality of a bag depends on something more subtle – the way the leather is cut (one or more layers at a time), the skill of the machinist in making invisible joins, the type of seams (piped, saddle-stitched, etc.) and the way the different

pieces, which must be pared (thinned) at the seams, are assembled. But good-quality leather is, of course, an essential component of any expensive article.

LEGATORIA

In the 19th century, many wealthy English people chose to live in fine villas on the outskirts of Florence. They were great travellers and asked bookbinders to make them luxurious leather-covered albums in which to keep their souvenirs, as well as notebooks for their travel notes and drawings. The house of Pineider, in the Piazza

THE FLAVOURS OF TUSCANY

Fragrant olive oil, meat full of flavour, vegetables in season, delicious charcuterie, aromatic herbs, ewe's milk cheeses and fine wines – all these local products are the ingredients of simple, tasty, country cooking that appeals to the taste buds. Some recipes are said to have been handed down from mother to daughter since Etruscan times. This shows how firmly the tradition of good food is rooted in the Tuscan soil.

RENAISSANCE RECIPES

When the young Catherine de Medici, fiancée of the future King Henry II, arrived in France in 1533, she was not alone. In her suite, an army of chefs and kitchen hands took possession of the Louvre kitchens. Besides the use of the fork, which was at that time unknown in her barbarous new land, some Tuscan recipes, including duck with orange *(Anitra all'arancia)*, were such a success that they came to be considered typically French. *Carabaccia* (onion soup thickened with ground almonds and flavoured with cinnamon), one of the Medicis' favourite dishes, is still eaten in Florence today.

CUCINA POVERA

One of the main qualities of Tuscan cuisine is that it uses only local products. There's a very good reason for this. The country people of Tuscany couldn't afford to buy expensive imported products, which is why chestnut flour forms the base of many desserts. The special flavour of Tuscan pork is due to the beechnuts on which the pigs are fed, while pine nuts, wild herbs and mushrooms are freely used in cooking. Unsalted bread, the staple food, is an ingredient of many dishes, such as *minestra di pane*, *panzanella* and *ribollita*.

ANTIPASTI

Besides the countless varieties of pasta – long *(spaghetti)*, in ribbons *(tagliatelle* and *fettucine)*, in smooth or fluted tubes *(penne)*, fancy *(farfalle* and *fusilli)* or stuffed *(ravioli, tortellini* and *cannelloni)* – that precede the main course, Tuscan meals traditionally start with the delicious local charcuterie.

Try the wild boar ham and sausage *(cinghiale)*, which are specialities of Maremma, or go for the more difficult to find *prosciutto casalingo sotto cenere*, which is ham buried under wood ash for a period of anything up to two years.

BEANS IN ABUNDANCE

The old Tuscan saying *Fiorentin mangia fagioli, lecca piatti e tavogliolo*, 'a Florentine who eats beans licks the plates and the tablecloths', is still as true today. Haricot beans are eaten all year round, fresh or dried. Cooked with olive oil, garlic, fresh sage and

ESSENTIAL EATING

One of the most celebrated Tuscan dishes is *bistecca alla Fiorentina*, a huge rib of beef (a special cut from the *chianina* breed), cooked on embers with a trickle of olive oil. If you're fond of tripe, *trippa alla fiorentina* (tripe with tomato and parmesan) will be a real find, as will *fritto misto*. This is a mixture of brain croquettes, calves' sweetbreads, artichokes, courgettes and lamb chops, which are all rolled in flour

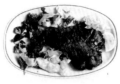

and beaten egg, fried and then browned in oil.

very ripe tomatoes (*all'Uccelletto*), they can be eaten hot or cold. *Ribollita*, the famous bean soup made from boiled beans, leeks, carrots, tomatoes, celery, black cabbage, garlic and thyme, is a hearty dish eaten in winter with black bread and fruity oil.

EXTRA VERGINE

Olive oil produced in Tuscany can be recognised by its yellowish-green colour and fruity flavour. The olives are harvested in the autumn when they're still green. They're then ground into a thick paste, spread on basketwork trays piled on top of one another

EAT YOUR WAY TO LONG LIFE

Mediterranean people live longer than those in the north. Their secret? A daily diet of virgin olive oil. This oil, from the first pressing of the olive, contains a monounsaturated fatty acid, oleic acid, that lowers the level of cholesterol in the blood while raising the level of unsaturated fat. Kept unopened in a cool, dark place, olive oil keeps for two years, otherwise it should be used within four months for the best flavour.

and cold-pressed. Once the plant water and paste residues have been removed, the fragrant liquid left is extra-virgin olive oil. When we take into account that olive trees only bear fruit every two years and aren't frost-hardy, that olives are picked by hand and that 5kg/11lb of olives have to be pressed to obtain a litre of oil, it's easy to see why it's so expensive.

TERRACOTTA, MAJOLICA, FAIENCE AND PORCELAIN

The term 'majolica' was first used in Italy at the end of the 15th century to designate the gold-tinged pottery made in Spain in Malaga, and later Valencia, and imported into Italy by Majorcan boats. While the name *maiolica* is generic in Italy and is used to designate any type of ceramic covered with opaque enamel, it's reserved by specialists for the whole of the faience produced in Italy up to the end of the Renaissance, whatever its type of decoration.

A TECHNIQUE OF MOSLEM ORIGIN

Whether the word *maiolica* is derived from Malaga (*Malaqa* in Arabic) or Majorca (Mallorca), it underlines the role played by Moorish Spain in the growth of a process that originated in the Near East. The technique for making tin-based opaque and white enamelled ceramics appeared in the 8th century and spread through the Mediterranean basin at the time of the Moslem conquests. It arrived in Spain enriched with a process perfected by the Fatimids of Egypt, the metallic lustre that gives majolica a golden bronze appearance. This is obtained by coating a piece that has already been fired and decorated, with metallic salts which, in the course of a second firing, give it a kind of iridescence varying in colour from green to coppery-red.

FAIENCE AND PORCELAIN

Faience is, by definition, a clay ceramic covered in a tin-based opaque white enamel. It made the potters of Faenza, from which it got its name *(bianchi di Faenza),* famous. The technique originated in Persia in response to the call for Chinese porcelain, which was transparent, hard and resonous, despite being made of clay. Moslem, (and later European) potters endlessly sought to reproduce it and their quest only ended in 1710 in Meissen, the first European factory to make porcelain from a hard paste.

THE MEDICI PORCELAIN

The first Chinese porcelain arrived in Europe via Italy in the 15th century, and it was in Florence, in the reign of Grand Duke Francesco I (1574-1587) that ceramists succeeded in making the first pieces of soft porcelain. This hybrid protoporcelain, made from a frit (a vitreous substance used in making porcelain or glazes) containing a little kaolin, was decorated with blue

THE DELLA ROBBIA STUDIO IN FLORENCE

Florence is, with Faenza, the oldest centre of majolica manufacture. We are probably indebted to Vasari for the association of the name of the Della Robbia studio with the invention of majolica. Luca Della Robbia (1482) was, in reality, first and foremost a famous sculptor who was the first to cover his terracotta works with an opaque, coloured enamel in order to give them brilliance and strength. The colours most often used were white and blue set off with green, yellow and pink. The studio was taken over by his nephew Andrea and his sons, who produced unique pieces up to the end of the 16th century.

DECORATIVE IDEAS

Around 1425, the original oriental-style blue and white decoration was replaced by a Gothico-floral style that often featured animals and the busts of people. In the late 15th century, decoration with artistic designs *(a istoriato)* rivalling painting was more in fashion. In the 16th century,

the Montelupo and Cafaggiolo factories near Florence, produced ceramics of great delicacy characterised by grotesque and fantastical motifs. They also excelled in pieces *a porcellana*, which imitated the Chinese 'blue and white' porcelain. In the 17th century, Montelupo ceramics were distinguished by their floral motifs and brilliant colours, including purplish-brown, leaf green, yellow, orange and turquoise.

oriental and European-inspired designs. The details of its manufacture were a jealously-guarded secret, and it wasn't until 1735 that porcelain was reborn in Italy in the Ginori à Doccia factory, where production has continued uninterrupted to the present day.

ITALIAN DESIGN

In the fifties, the Italians made a noted entry into the world of contemporary design with revolutionary materials and original shapes. Half a century later, they're still noted for their avant-garde design, continuing to innovate with humour and flair, while the hallmark designs of the golden age, such as the Vespa and Fiat Cinquecento, are as popular as ever.

DOMUS

The Milanese architect Gio Ponti, who founded the review *Domus* in 1928, was the first to understand the importance of a magazine specialising in the field of everyday objects, furniture and industrial production. From the fifties

onwards, the review was entirely devoted to Italian design, reflecting the necessity for reviving industry to find new outlets on the basis of both the functionality and the beauty of an object.

FUTURISTIC MATERIALS

The Italian designers were the first to introduce new materials into our everyday lives. In 1951, polyurethane foam made its appearance at the Milan Triennial, opening up a whole new world of possibilities in terms of line, structure and industrial-scale production. Sofas were transformed into voluptuous lips or Ionic capitals, and coat racks became giant cactuses. After PVC and fibreglass, the Italians made use of titanium and carbon

fibre, materials that are both strong and light.

INFLATABLE FURNITURE

The 'Up' armchairs designed by Gaetano Pesce in 1969 were sold vacuum sealed in a flat pack, reduced to a tenth of their volume. When removed from their packaging, they auto-inflated and returned to their original size. At the same time, the manufacturer Zanotta launched an inflatable PVC chair onto the market. According to the publicity blurb it was 'a big doll that embraced you and sat you on its lap'. The fashion for inflatables is now back with a vengeance with a whole stack of objects that can float or be inflated according to need – very practical if you live in a small flat.

THE FLORENTINE SCHOOL

In the mid-sixties, the Superstudio and Archizoom groups which emerged from the Florentine Academy of Architecture rebelled against the fact that designers were becoming the servants of industry. From their utopian plans for the division of space emerged ideas that would be exploited by

Andrea Branzi, Massimo Morozzi and Paolo Deganello in the seventies and eighties. Among these were the famous Tangram table designed by Morozzi in 1983, composed of modules of the Chinese game of the same name, and the Aeo armchair (Deganello, 1973), which could be completely taken to pieces, with the frames of the seat and back fitting into the plastic foot.

TANTALISING TABLEWARE

From 1983 onwards, thanks to the Alessi firm's project entitled *Tea and Coffee Piazza,* famous architects could give form to their fantasies. Among the many designs, tending in general towards gadgetry, some

stand out above the rest– a tray in the shape of an aircraft carrier and a coffeepot with aggressively sober lines by Hans Holbein, and the Ti Tang coffeepot by Philippe Starck, now a design classic. The current line in stainless steel or plastic by talented young designers, such as Andrea Castiglioni and Carla Ceccariglia, is mainly designed for fun.

BEST SELLERS

The Fiat Cinquecento, the ideal car designed by Giacosa in 1957, has a large fan club in Japan. The Vespa (or 'wasp') designed by an aeronautical engineer, Corradino d'Ascanio just after the Second World War, is still making a fortune for its manufacturer Piaggio. The Plia chair (transparent,

folding and considered to be essential), designed by Giancarlo Piretti and first produced by Castelli in 1969, can be found in every home. Lastly, the Brionvega radio designed in 1965 is still in production today.

MARZIO CECCHI

Several designs by the brilliant architect and decorator, Marzio Cecchi (who died prematurely in 1979), can be seen in Florence (the Cavour hotel, and the Beltrami and Casadei shops). Having trained at the Florentine school of architecture, he showed himself to be one of the most inventive designers of

his day. He designed furniture that was both personal and timeless in which the fabric played a predominant role, including the blue furniture of St Julien's golf course, Deauville, and unique pieces that are still sold by Studio Most in Florence (p. 114).

THE CRADLE OF THE RENAISSANCE

At the end of the Middle Ages, which had been shaken by epidemics and political and religious crises, a new order was imposed by the Medicis. Combined with a growing awareness of a rich past and the birth of a humanist philosophy, it created a favourable climate for the dawn of a new creative movement known as the *Rinascità*. This was based in Florence for a whole century, the *quattrocento,* before emigrating to Rome, where it renewed its vigor in the Baroque period.

Cosimo de' Medici or Cosimo the Elder (1389-1464)

PROUD TO BE FLORENTINE

Leonardo Bruni, a humanist and the chancellor of Florence in 1410, epitomised a state of mind still prevalent among Florentines today, namely a belief in their superiority over other Italians. This conviction allowed Florentine society to reach new heights of creative and artistic achievement, that are still remarkable five centuries later.

The Gates of Paradise *(Baptistery)*

THE MAJOR SITES

The middle classes, enriched by the cloth trade and banking, were responsible for financing the construction of religious and secular buildings designed to exalt the power of Florence. A competition launched to decide who would make the doors of the Baptistery was won by Ghiberti. His rival, Brunelleschi, was given the job of crowning the unfinished cathedral with a cupola whose perfection was to be a symbol of the Renaissance. The corporations ordered statues of their patron saints from the best sculptors to decorate the niches of Orsanmichele church.

ACTIVE PATRONAGE

Florence is as much indebted for its culture to the enemies of Cosimo de'Medici as to the grand duke and his friends. But it's to Cosimo that we owe the discovery of Donatello's genius, the setting up of a library for scholars at the convent of San Marco and the magnificent collection of statues, reliefs and ancient medallions that were used as models by artists. It was he, too, who ordered frescoes from Fra Angelico for the convent of San Marco and from Gozzoli for his palace, protected Filippo Lippi from the severity of the pope and entrusted Michelozzo with the building of his palace and many villas. Far more than his grandson, Lorenzo, it was Cosimo who contributed to the birth of the Renaissance.

VANISHING POINT

It was his obsession with perspective that made Uccello get up in the middle of the night to study mathematics. To reproduce the world as the eye sees it and produce a perfect illusion of the three dimensional world was the

THE NEW GOLDEN AGE

The renewed interest in Antiquity that occurred at the end of the 14th century gathered pace in 1453 when Greek scholars chased from Constantinople by the Turks arrived in Italy.

Ucello: The Battle of San Romano

preoccupation of the Renaissance artists who invented central perspective. Alberti spoke of it in his treatise on painting, Brunelleschi created the optical box, Uccello and Andrea del Castagno geometrised space, and Donatello created *schiacciato*, graded reliefs giving the illusion of depth in a small thickness.

They brought with them unknown manuscripts, original versions of ancient works and knowledge that revolutionised Italian ways of thinking. Impressed by their learning, Cosimo the Elder gave his villa at Careggi to Marsile Ficin, who founded the Platonic Academy there, bringing together all the scholars of the day.

HUMANISM INCARNATE

Alberti, who applied his theories on the rules of proportion of Classical Antiquity to the façades of Santa Maria Novella and the Palazzo Rucellai, was the first dilettante architect of the Renaissance. He embodied the ideal of the universal man and was a fine rider and athlete, a composer and playwright and a jurist of the first order, who also painted and studied the mathematical and physical sciences. His treatises on painting and architecture were used as reference books by several generations of artists.

Detail of the façade of the Church of Santa Maria Novella

THE RENAISSANCE MASTERS

The Renaissance masters, who were natives of Florence or the surrounding countryside, were the architects of a movement that spread throughout Italy and beyond its frontiers. To study the Antiquity they admired so much, they travelled to Rome and frequented the Casino Mediceo, a garden behind San Marco, where the antique statues and reliefs bought by the Medicis were assembled. Three generations of artists, sculptors, painters and architects, from Donatello to Michelangelo, Masaccio to Leonardo da Vinci and Brunelleschi to Buontalenti, set a seal of beauty on Florence.

Donatello: David

A FOUR-HANDED RENAISSANCE

Donatello and Brunelleschi, one a sculptor and the other an architect, were lifelong friends. Together they studied the ancient monuments of Rome, an experience that strongly marked their production, and worked on the most prestigious sites in Florence. It was a dialogue that lasted forty years. You can read about it in the old sacristy (vestry) of San Lorenzo, where the reliefs on the arches form an integral part of the structure. Brunelleschi is known mainly for the cupola (dome) of the Duomo, which was built without scaffolding, as well as the harmonious proportions of the Hospital of the Innocents and San Spirito. He infused his statuary with such intensity of expression that he would be a master for future generations.

GHIBERTI AND THE GOLDSMITHS

In 1425, Lorenzo Ghiberti received a commission on which he was to work for twenty-five years – the east door of the Baptistery, which Michelangelo was later to liken to the Gates of Paradise. Besides great technical ability, he displayed a perfect under-standing of ancient art, combined with an astute grasp of perspective, which allowed him to achieve the illusion of depth in both landscapes and architectural representations. Goldsmith-ing, ever closely linked with wealth, also underwent considerable expansion elsewhere, especially in the

Ghiberti: Panel from the Gates of Paradise *(Baptistery)*

production of medallions, an art in which Antonio Pollaiolo excelled.

MASACCIO AND FRA ANGELICO, BETWEEN REALITY AND MYSTICISM

Fra Angelico: Coronation of the Virgin *(detail)*

Strong, realistic figures, highlighted with dramatic lighting, and the recreation of a three-dimensional landscape with his use of perspective (a vanishing point situated at eye level), made Masaccio the true pioneer of expressive painting. In contrast with this, Fra Angelico, despite having accepted certain new principles such as perspective, desired above all to touch the spectator's soul by means of gilding and luminous colours.

FROM THE LINE TO *SFUMATO*

A pupil of Filippo Lippi, the Carmelite brother who painted pictures of the Virgin with a pagan beauty, Botticelli was the master of drawing. In his work, the forms are precise and the lines flow and take on an almost poetic freedom. His paintings are a mixture of the sacred and profane subjects, mythology and neo-Platonism. With Leonardo da Vinci,

several years his junior, an art form born half a century earlier came to maturity. Having realised that the eye has difficulty in perceiving shape and can no longer identify colour from a distance, he dissolved outlines

LEONARDO DA VINCI

and unified colours in a hazy atmosphere that he named *sfumato*.

THE SOLITARY GENIUS

Michelangelo, who was both an architect and a painter, only really fulfilled himself in sculpture, in which he best expressed his *terribilità* (a contained violence, translated by anxiety that lead his hand towards creating more and more tormented shapes). Florence possesses a large number of his works, which show the development of an artist who set out to equal the Creator. From his muscular David to the moving sketches of his final years, he interpreted the great human drama like no other artist.

Michelangelo in his studio (19th-century painting)

THE MEDICI SAGA

The nouveau riche Medicis came from humble origins and by means of intrigue, succeeded in becoming the uncontested masters of Florence in just two generations. But these formidable bankers were also fervent humanists who, through active patronage, helped to make Florence the foremost art city of the Renaissance. These former merchants were elevated to the rank of grand dukes, and members of the family became popes, cardinals and, on two occasions, queens of France.

Giovanni de' Medici (1475-1521), who became Pope Leo X, was the son of Lorenzo the Magnificent

BANKER TO THE POPES

Giovanni di Bicci (1360-1429) started the family fortune. His ancestors were rude peasants from Mugello, who, in the late 12th century, moved to the San Lorenzo district, a parish to which the Medicis remained faithful. At first merchants, they later became moneylenders. Giovanni, who had branches in Genoa, Bruges, Venice and Rome, managed the papal finances while carrying on international trade in wool, pewterware and luxury goods. He also made himself a name in politics by taking care to offend no-one. On his death he left his son Cosimo 178,221 florins and a vast fortune in real estate.

COSIMO, THE FATHER OF THE NATION

A mediocre orator but a shrewd businessman, a manipulator but also a friend of the arts, Cosimo managed to turn a republican state attached to its liberties into a principality in fact, if not in name. Avoiding all obvious signs of wealth (though he did have the Palazzo Medici-Riccardi

built), he proclaimed himself to be an ordinary citizen and rarely occupied the highest offices in thirty years. He eliminated his political enemies by banishment and the confiscation of their goods, which enriched the Medicis' allies. These shrewd policies earned him on his death the ancient title of *Pater Patriae*.

LORENZO THE MAGNIFICENT

On 1 January 1449, Lucrezia Tornabuoni gave birth to a son who was baptised Lorenzo. He was barely twenty when he succeeded his father, Piero the Gouty (Cosimo's son), and was to become the man who really epitomised the ideals of the Florentine humanists . This new prince, who was olive-skinned, with bulging eyes and a prominent jaw, had very refined tastes. He was a patron of the arts, and a great womaniser, but could also show a cruel side to his nature. The Pazzis and

DOCTORS OR BANKERS?

Some people have thought that the round bezants *(palle)* adorning the Medici arms were pills indicating the presence of doctors *(medici)* or apothecaries among their ancestors. *'Palle!'* was also the cry given by the Medicis' clients when they threw themselves into the fray. However, it's more

realistic to suppose the bezants repesented gold coins, the emblem of bankers. The arms' original eleven bezants were reduced to seven, and later six, including an azure one, adorned with the lily of France, an honour conferred on Piero the Gouty by Louis XI of France.

The preacher Savonarole was the Medicis' fiercest critic

of Naples and annexation of Milan, Charles V promised to restore the Medicis to Florence. However, they were from then on strictly controlled by Spanish garrisons.

GRAND DUKES OF TUSCANY

Alexander, the natural son of Pope Clement VII who was enobled by the emperor, only distinguished himself by his greed, debauchery and violent behaviour. Assassinated by his cousin Lorenzo (Alfred de Musset's *Lorenzaccio*), he was succeeded by Cosimo, who consolidated the alliance with Spain by marrying the beautiful Eleonora of Toledo. Ambitious and brutal, he muzzled the old aristocracy, kept order with the help of a secret police force and wouldn't rest until he was recognised as one of the foremost princes of Italy. Catherine, Lorenzo the Magnificent's only direct descendant, was married at the age of sixteen to Henry, Duke of Orleans, and the Florentine Republic was over, for once and for all.

their accomplices, who in 1478 mounted an assassination attempt that cost his younger brother Giuliano his life, discovered it to their cost. Their bodies were left swinging from the windows of the Palazzo Vecchio to serve as an example to anyone who might question his authority again.

THE RETURN OF THE MEDICIS

Driven out of Florence by the monk Savonarole, who preached divine anger against a city dedicated to money-making and pleasure, the Medicis made a triumphant return in 1530. The way for their return had been paved by two popes – Leo X, the son of Lorenzo the Magnificent, and Clement VII, Giuliano's illegitimate son. In return for Clement VII's agreement to his investiture with the Kingdom

The nephew of Lorenzo the Magnificent, Giulio de' Medici, who became Pope Clement VII, triggered the Anglican schism by exccommunicating King Henry VIII

COUNTRY LIFE: VILLAS AND GARDENS

In the early 16th century, the fortified rural estate became a holiday villa, with sumptuous gardens, where banquets and festivities took place. The worship of life, nature and beauty was the ideal of

Villa Gameraia at Settignano

Florentine patricians, who spent long periods at their beautiful villas. These country houses opened onto vast gardens cooled by fountains, close to forests where roe deer and wild boar were hunted. Perched on the hills around Florence, some of the Medici villas have retained their bucolic charm.

THE MEDICIS USHER IN THE COUNTRY HOUSE

Cosimo the Elder was the first to entrust the architect Michelozzo with the task of refurbishing his properties at Trebbio and Cafaggiolo in his native Mugello. The fortified rural estates were turned into pleasant holiday homes, where the Medicis received their protégés – philosophers, scholars and artists. Though each villa still had a watch tower and defences left over from more turbulent times, it now centred on an interior courtyard embellished with porticoes on the ground floor and a loggia on the first. There were numerous windows that let in plenty of light and gave views out onto the magnificent gardens, which formed a link with the surrounding countryside.

The Apennine Colossus *in the garden of the Villa Demidoff*

A GALLERY OF MASTERPIECES

The Medicis set a trend by asking the best artists to decorate their villas. The *Birth of Venus* and *Spring*, Botticelli's two most famous paintings, were hung in the Medici villa at Castello. Giambologna was the creator of the Fountain of Venus at the Villa Petraia at Castello, as well as the remarkable

Apennine Colossus adorning the garden of the Villa Demidoff at Pratolino. Finally, Andrea del Sarto and Pontormo painted large frescoes illustrating the lives of the Medicis in the drawing room of the Villa Poggio at Caiano.

THE OPENING OF THE SECRET GARDEN

The garden, an integral part of the Tuscan villa, evolved along with the architecture. Adjacent to the house, the small enclosed medieval garden, or *giardino segreto*, corresponded to the humanist

The Villa Demidoff

ideal of nature that has been tamed. Next to the orchard and the kitchen garden beds of flowers and aromatic herbs were planted, while the water splashing in the fountains and vine-covered arbours provided cool refreshment in summer.

THE ITALIAN GARDEN

The extension of the garden, which merged with the villa, obeyed strict laws of perspective and geometry involving the polarity of the four elements. Straight paths lined with cypresses, lemon

trees planted in pots and immaculately trimmed box hedges, with semicircular ponds and terraces to close the view, all characterised the Italian garden of the period.

This succession of formal, architectural planting was cultivated next to a wooded section which was left in its natural state.

THEATRES OF GREENERY

In the 16th century the garden was the preferred setting for many of the amusements of the Florentine society, a society fond of fireworks and open-air entertainment of all kinds. Staircases were often the key elements of these spectacular productions and it became necessary to call on the work of architects and designers. The landscape gardener Tribolo and the architect Buontalenti, who most notably designed the Boboli gardens, laid out terraced gardens dotted with

fountains, where mock grottoes, allegorical statues and mazes held many a surprise for those out walking.

STONE PAINTINGS

The craze for semiprecious stone marquetry, inherited from the Romans, has left its mark on the Florentine landscape. It can be seen in the multicoloured façades of the churches, the sumptuous paving, the gleaming mosaics and even the priceless furniture in the palaces. This constantly developing art is still one of the jewels of the Florentine craft tradition.

Colour chart of semiprecious stones (Ugolini)

A SCHOOL FOR MOSAICISTS

The start of work on the Baptistery in the early 13th century

marked the opening of a Florentine school for mosaicists. They were probably trained by craftsmen from Venice, where the art had continued uninterrupted since ancient times. While the techniques remained the same – namely the insertion of small cubes of marble and coloured glass in fresh mortar – the collaboration of as famous an artist as Cimabue, who drew the sketches that inspired the craftsmen, was something new.

MULTI-COLOURED FAÇADES

To decorate the churches, the ancient monuments were relentlessly stripped. Columns made from porphyry (a marble containing crystals) were cut up into decorative discs and white marble chancels were incorporated in new geometrical designs. When supplies ran out, the old quarries, abandoned since the time of the Roman Empire, were put back into production. Every shade of marble – white marble from Carrara, pink marble from Maremma and dark green marble from Prato – adorns the façades and paving of the Duomo, Santa Maria Novella and the marvellous little church of San Miniato al Monte.

PURPLE PASSION

When he became duke of Tuscany after the sudden death of his brother Francesco, ex-cardinal Ferdinando de' Medici renounced the purple and satisfied his passion for the colour by surrounding himslf with Egyptian porphyry. He re-established the special technique for cutting this very hard marble (using water and abrasives). In 1588 he founded the Opificio delle Pietre Dure, a workshop entirely devoted to the cutting of semiprecious stones, which reveal remarkable patterns of flowers or coloured waves when cut into very fine slices.

THE COMMESSO FIORENTINO

Rock crystal cutters, brought from Milan, perfected the

technique of *commesso*, the art of making pictures from stones carefully chosen for their colour and texture. Whether it was a landscape or a floral composition, the craftsman's skill lay in choosing the thousand and one shades and gradations of colour, as well as the effects of transparency and opacity of the stones. Small fragments of the cut stones were then set in trays of black granite or stuck on slate supports before being polished. The finished effect was often breathtaking.

A LUXURY ART

These durable compositions, which often had skillful perspectives, elaborate lines and baroque skies, were much

sought after by the princes of Europe, who ordered them from the Opificio delle Pietre Dure. Besides stone pictures, the factory produced tabletops, tops for chests of drawers, vases and a variety of very expensive objects, each of which required between two and sixteen years' work. A lack of wealthy clients forced the Opificio delle Pietre Dure to cease production around 1880, when it was converted into a museum and stone restoration centre.

Traditional compositon on an Egyptian porphyry table (Ugolini)

malachite from Siberia, black nephrite and red sard from Egypt, jasper streaked with green from Bohemia, orange-coloured chalcedony from the Orient and blue lapis lazuli from Persia. See their unique collection at the museum of the Opificio delle Pietre Dure (Via degli Alfani, 78 ☎ 055 21 01 02, open 9am-2pm, closed Sun. and holidays.

STONE OF EVERY SHADE

Although Tuscany offers a rich variety of coloured stone – striped jasper from the Arno, red agate and yellow marble from Siena, milky chalcedony and alabaster from Volterra – the Medicis used their agents to have stones imported from all over the world. The range of colours was then enriched with blue-tinted agates from Goa, green

PIETRA PAESINA

These fine-grained limestones, which originate from the area around Florence offer different patterns with every cut. Infiltrations of water-bearing mineral salts, especially iron oxide and manganese, were the cause of these patterns, which were millions of years in the making.

FESTIVE FLORENCE

Colourful jousts, magnificent processions and dazzling firework displays were a regular feature of Florentine life during the Renaissance. Though austere Florence is less talked about than its rival Siena or flamboyant Venice, its inhabitants are still passionate in their celebration of the *Scoppio del Carro* and *Calcio,* two festivals of pagan origin that welcome in the spring and start of summer. Witnessing one of these events will give you a better understanding of the very soul of Florence.

A CITY OF PLEASURE

Lorenzo and Giuliano de' Medici were masters in the art of organising festivities. The tournament of January 1475 was long remembered. It was held in honour of Giuliano's mistress, Simonetta Cattaneo, whose beauty inspired Botticelli to paint his Venus (*The Birth of Venus*, in the Uffizi). Throughout the year there were large processions with allegorical themes taken from tales of chivalry or mythology. Masked horseman would ride through the city, stopping in the squares to take part in jousts and perform pantomimes or theatrical speeches with musical accompaniments that were often written by Lorenzo the Magnificent himself.

THE SCOPPIO DEL CARRO

On Easter Day, people crowd round the Duomo to witness the *Scoppio del Carro* ('Explosion of the Carriage'). A procession made up of representatives of Florence's oldest families, dressed in historical costumes, follows a huge wooden carriage packed with rockets drawn by four white oxen. When it arrives

Botticelli: The Birth of Venus *(Uffizi)*

in front of the cathedral, it stops at the portals which are left wide open. Suddenly, at the chanting of the Gloria, a mechanical dove shoots up from the high altar, fizzes along a wire and sets the chariot ablaze. It's a crucial moment, since the abundance of the summer harvest is said to depend on the success of the fireworks.

THE CALCIO

St John's Day (devoted to the city's patron saint) was once, with New Year's Day (at that time 25 March), one of the Florentines' best-loved and popular celebrations. The procession of sixteen district standards ended in the Piazza Santa Croce. Here, the *Calcio* joust, which pitted the various *rione* (medieval districts) of Florence against one another, was held. The *Calcio Storico*, which is played in three stages round the summer solstice (19, 24 and 28 June), still takes place in the same setting. Teams of 27 players, dressed in their district colours, meet

in a merciless battle that's a mixture of football, rugby and Roman wrestling. The prize is a white calf and, of course, for the victorious *rione*, the honour of winning. Before every match there are processions in 16th-century costume, with the nobility mounted on elaborately dressed horses and 500 extras marching to the sound of trumpets and drums. The show ends with a magnificent firework display in the Piazzale Michelangelo.

THE OTHER FESTIVALS

The New Year opens with a *canottieri* (rowers') competition, followed by a parade of small boats on the Arno (1 January). In May, on the first Sunday after Ascension, every household buys a lucky cricket in a little cage. As a prelude to the *Calcio*, the four districts take part in a rowing race on the Arno (*Palio remiero*) in early June. On 10 August a banquet is held in front of the church of San Lorenzo in honour of the Medicis' patron saint. September is the children's month and they congregate in the Piazza della Santa Annunziata on the Virgin's birthday (7 August) all holding coloured paper lanterns (*festa della Rificolona*). Around the middle of December, cribs

(*presepe*) are set up all over the city and the year ends in style with Christmas mass and the feast of *Capodanno*, or New Year's Day.

LAVORARE IN MURO: THE SECRETS OF FRESCO PAINTING

Fresco (late 19th century) in the cathedral of Florence

The extraordinary freshness of the Renaissance frescoes revealed by the patient work of the restorers over the last few decades has given rise to some controversy. We had, after all, become accustomed to seeing their dusky beauty veiled in dust and dirt. Frescoes have nevertheless acquired such renown that the word is now used to denote any mural painting. Yet painting on fresh (*fresco*) plaster requires such skill that the technique was gradually abandoned after the 17th century in favour of painting on a dry (*secco*) surface, which is quicker but less durable.

PAINTING AND FRESCO PAINTING

In his *Libro dell'arte,* published in 1430, Cennino Cennini was the first to discuss the technique of fresco painting. Before him, the theoretician Alberti failed to consider the work of the fresco painter worthy of inclusion in his treatise on painting. Unlike a painter working at his own speed in a studio, a fresco painter perched on scaffolding had to put up with changes in the light around him and the

Ceiling of the loggia of the Ospedale degli Innocenti

inconvenience of plaster dust, while working quickly on a damp wall.

THE PRELIMINARIES: *ARRICIO* AND *SINOPIA*

After the wall had been covered in a first layer of rough mortar (the *arricio*), it was divided into squares by drawing straight lines with a cord dipped in red paint *(battere il filo)*. This guided the painter's hand as he sketched the broad lines of the composition with red earth, hence the name *sinopia* which is given to this preliminary drawing. In the

15th century, this practice was gradually replaced by the projection of powdered charcoal *(spolvero)* onto a perforated sketch, or by transferring the outline by means of incisions.

A DAY'S WORK

Before adding the *intonaco* (the smooth, very fine-grained layer of plaster), it was necessary to decide how much work could be done in a day *(giornata)*. Colours obtained by dissolving earth and minerals in water were applied to fresh damp plaster. As they

Fresco by Vasari in Santa Maria dei Fiore

Frescoed ceiling (19th century) in the Palazzo Pitti

dried, they formed a strong, tough amalgam. It was in this last, delicate phase that the artist's talent became apparent. Apart from the fact that he alter his painting, he had to know what the final shade of the colours (which changed when they dried) would be and avoid over-visible joints between the different *giornate*.

FINIRE IN SECCO

To mask such defects, most painters touched up their work once it was dry with pigments of a different kind which, when mixed with organic binders (yolk or white of egg) as an agglutinant, gave the composition a more intense luminosity. These less stable colours have often faded or even disappeared due to the action of the light, revealing the fresco in all its admirable imperfection.

FRESCOES WITHOUT A WALL

In the late 18th century, in order to conserve them or out of simple curiosity, frescoes were moved by means of a *stacco*. A thick canvas was stuck onto the fresco which allowed the painted layer to be removed. This was then placed on another support (concrete or canvas). This technique has two major drawbacks: the loss of anything painted *a secco* (after the plaster has dried) when the canvas is removed, and the loss of the colours which, in the absence of the important layer of plaster, fade before your very eyes. Nowadays, frescoes are only moved in cases of absolute necessity, such as the flood of the Arno in 1966, which caused the loss of 3,000m²/ 32,000sqft of frescoes. Those that could be saved were detached from the wall by an *intonaco* (*stacco* method).

IN SITU

The new school of restorers deals with the problem as a

whole – conserving the monument, cleaning the frescoes and protecting them from deterioration due to damp and pollution, as well as malicious damage by visitors. It took six years' of painstaking work to restore the frescoes of the Brancacci Chapel to their original freshness. The restoration of the *Procession of the Three Wise Men*, by Benozzo Gozzoli, in the chapel of the Palazzo Medici-Riccardi, was completed in 1994 after four years' painstaking labour. But the result was definitely worth waiting for.

Fresco by Perugino in the sacristy of the Pazzi Chapel (see p. 59)

THE ART OF WEAVING WOOL, SILK AND COTTON

In the Middle Ages, the Arte de Calimala (Drapers' Guild) was the most powerful in Florence. Its speciality was the finishing of fabrics imported from across the mountains, which were subsequently sold at a considerably higher price. Two other guilds came to the fore in the early 14th century, the Arte de Lana (Wool Guild) and Arte de Seta (Silk Guild). Despite the textile crisis caused by English and Dutch competition, their workshops remain open to this day.

THE *ARTE DE CALIMALA*

In a street of ill repute in Florence, the Via Calimala *(Calis Malus),* Florentine

merchants grew rich on the woollen cloth trade, because they possessed the secret of a dressing and dyeing process that turned rough Flemish and French woollen cloth into sumptuous fabrics that only the princes of Europe could afford. The untreated cloth was distributed among the various guilds who then fulled, pressed, smoothed and cut it. To dye it, they used woad (blue), madder (red) and dyer's moss (crimson), and several families, including the Rucellai, grew wealthy by importing these plants.

THE MAJOR ARTS

In the late 12th century, a number of guilds detached themselves from the Arte de Calimala – the money-changers, silk workers, wool workers, skinners and furriers, doctors and apothecaries, and judges and notaries. These seven guilds, the Major Arts, were run by the upper middle class, and each had its own palace, arms and standard. The wool workers soon became the most important, and by the middle of the 14th century were producing 100,000

pieces of cloth in their 300 workshops, which employed a third of the city's population.

THE WOOL AND SILK GUILDS

Wool was imported from England, Portugal and Spain, while the indispensable alum ore came first from Morea and later, after the Turkish invasion, from the Voterra and Tolfa deposits, when it was the cause of serious disputes. Young men were sent to trade in Europe and the Orient, from where they brought

back precious silks that were hastily imitated. In the 15th century Florence surpassed the Orient in the manufacture of brocades – sumptuous fabrics made from silk interwoven

with raised gold and silver threads. All the great Florentine families owned their own workshops where silk cloth with personalised designs was made. It was used to make clothes, but above all was used as a furnishing fabric.

ANTICO SETIFICO FIORENTINO

While the woollen industry went into a marked decline in the 17th century, silk production continued to increase. The Guicciardinis, Della Gherardescas, Puccis, Corsinis and other illustrious families pooled their looms,

point papers and designs to create a single workshop in the Via dei Tessitori. Here, they mainly produced silk fabric with which to decorate their palaces and chapels or make flags at festival time. But the demand from the European aristocracy was such that the workshop had to expand and move to the Via Bartolini. The hand looms still in use today are those presented by Grand Duke Peter-Leopold of Lorraine in 1780. (Via Bartolini, 4 ☎ 055 21 38 61, Mon.-Fri. 9am-1pm, 2-5pm, closed Aug.)

TESSITURA DI ROVEZZANO

In 1946, Countess Maria Antonietta di Frassineto decided to perpetuate the Florentine tradition of fine furnishing fabrics and installed a large weaving workshop, equipped with

antique mechanical looms, in her property at Rovezzano. The only example in Europe of pre-industrial civilisation, the workshop produces superb fabric made of Egyptian cotton which is sometimes mixed with linen or enhanced with discreet gold threads. The designs take their inspiration from paintings, frescoes and ancient tapestries, but can also be made to order to harmonise with your tableware or the colour of a carpet. You can admire these marvellous fabrics at Via Aretina, 507 ☎ 055 69 00 23, Mon.-Fri. 8.30am-12.30pm, 2-5.30pm (bus 14).

DAMASK

Damask, a fabric with ornamental patterns, was named after Damascus because its matt and satin designs are reminiscent of the glint of damascened metal, a speciality of the city. The cloth itself is monochrome and the design is made by the combination of a matt background and shiny patterns. Fully reversible, and manufactured in Europe since the 15th century, damask figures in almost all the great houses of the last few centuries. Made of silk or cotton, damask is still one of the specialities of Florentine workshops.

Old view of Florence from the Casa dei Tessutti (see p. 43)

THE MAGIC OF PERFUME

From their expeditions to the Orient, the crusaders brought back unknown spices and delicious fragrances from the fabrics in which relics were wrapped. Aromatic substances brought back in quantities by Florentine merchants as early as the 13th century were gradually included in cooking or used by monks for their curative properties. The alchemists of the Renaissance carried out further experiments, blending aromas to create perfumes that were soon adopted by elegant people of both sexes. This skillful art has been revived by Lorenzo Villoresi, who distills made-to-measure perfumes in his Florentine palace.

OFFICINA PROFUMO FARMACEUTICA

At Santa Maria Novella, as in all medieval convents, there was a small medicinal herb garden used to make potions and salves. Essences and resins, as well as distillation processes from the Orient, enriched their stock of drugs. People came from far and wide to buy rosewater (which was considered a disinfectant) alkermes (an elixir that rekindled the mind) tincture of myrrh (which cured bleeding gums) and the water of Santa Maria Novella (which helped digestion). This activity has continued uninterrupted until the present day, and the walls of the old pharmacy still exude exotic perfumes.

FLORENCE, THE PERFUME CAPITAL

The perfume craze swept the Renaissance courts. Lucrecia Borgia and Isabelle d'Este rivalled one another in the art

of inventing new perfumes. Francesco de' Medici, who was interested in alchemy and had a secret laboratory in the Palazzo Vecchio, perfected new fragrances between attempts at discovering the philosopher's stone. Leonardo da Vinci carried out research to improve the production techniques of the perfume industry, in particular 'enfleurage' (a process in which oils acquire fragrance

OCCUPATION: MASTER PERFUMER

Much-travelled ancestors, a thorough knowledge of Arab philosophy, a botanist father and a passionate interest in fragrances are the ingredients which have made Lorenzo Villoresi, a university researcher, a master perfumer, whose fame has crossed the Atlantic. He receives his clients on the top floor of the family palace on the banks of the river Arno. At the end of a conversation lasting two or three hours, a unique perfume is born and presented in a blue crystal bottle with a silver stopper. You can enjoy this delightful experience by appointment at Via de Bardi, 14, ☎ 055 234 11 87 ✆ 055 234 58 93. Besides made-to-measure perfumes, he makes marvellous pots-pourris, luxurious bath products and perfumed candles.

by being exposed to the scent of flowers). In the late 15th century compilations of recipes for medicines and perfumes were published for the first time, the *Ricettario Fiorentino* and the *Secreti Notandissimi dell'arte Profumatoria*.

THE IRIS, EMBLEM OF FLORENCE

Extract of iris, a powerful violet-scented and slightly woody concentrate used in the composition of many perfumes, is obtained by way of a lenghty process. Three-year-old iris rhizomes are washed and peeled, then left to dry for three more years, after which the rhizome powder is distilled for twenty hours. The yield is very low and it takes at least 100kg/220lb of rhizomes to produce 100gm/3½oz of essence, which explains its high cost, three times that of gold. In Tuscany, iris powder is often used to flavour Chianti, a practice dating back to Antiquity.

A FASHION FROM ITALY

Among the company of master perfumers and magicians who followed Catherine de' Medici to France was one Renato Bianco, better known by the name of René le Florentin, who opened a shop in the Rue du Pont-au-Change in Paris. It was another Florentine, Renato Tombarelli, who started the production of flowers for the perfume industry in Grasse. And so the fashion for perfuming the whole body,

in order to camouflage any unpleasant odours caused by a lack of hygiene, was propagated.

STOCK UP AT BIZZARRI

Though Florence lost its title of perfume capital in the 17th century, it still has a large number of extremely well-stocked herbalist's shops where you can find all kinds of plants, herbs, spices and cosmetic products made according to old recipes. The most amazing is the house of Bizzarri in the Via Condotta, which is not to be missed (p. 47).

Florence Practicalities

MOVING ABOUT THE CITY

You can easily get around the tourist districts of Florence on foot. The longest journeys take twenty minutes at most, since the important monuments and museums are contained within a square kilometre/half a square mile. In principle, the historic city centre is banned to traffic. The journey from the Duomo to the Ponte Vecchio by way of the Piazza della Signoria is more pleasant since the area has become pedestrianised, especially as the large number of shops *en route* means you can do some window shopping as you go from church to museum. A stroll before or after dinner is the favourite *passeggiata* (walk) of Florentine families. As you can imagine, it isn't a very good idea to drive round Florence in a car since, apart from the problem of

parking and understanding the direction of the traffic alongside the Arno, you have to cope with Italian driving and scooters dodging about in all directions. You may be able to get to the door of your hotel by car, but then you'll have to find somewhere safe and legal to park if you don't want it towed away or broken into – cars registered abroad are particularly prone to theft while they are parked. Lastly, bear in mind that hotels that have their own garages charge L30,000-40,000 a day for parking. Public car parks may charge a cheaper rate if you leave the car parked for 4 or 5 days, but charge according to engine capacity. In other words, it's cheaper to park a Fiat Uno than a Maserati!

ON TWO WHEELS

Florence isn't Rome, and you can be sure of a fine if you're caught riding with two people to a scooter. You need to allow L20,000 a day to hire a bike, L45,000 for a scooter and L80,000 for a motorbike and the helmet you're legally required to wear. You can leave your credit card number as a guarantee. Telephone in advance on Sundays to check the shop is open. Bike and scooter hire:

Ciao e Basta
Costa dei Magnoli, 24
☎ 055 29 62 30 (bikes).

Free Motor
Via Santa Monica, 6-8
☎ 055 29 51 02 (bikes).
Motorent
Via San Zanobi, 9r
☎ 055 49 01 13 (mountain bikes and scooters).
Vespa Rent
Via Pisana, 103
☎ 055 71 56 9 (scooters).
Alinari
Via Guelfa, 85r
☎ 055 28 05 00 (bikes, scooters and motorbikes).

BY BUS

Even if you can make sense of the bus map, which is no mean feat in itself, it won't be much help when it comes to moving round the city centre. Lines A and D have electric buses serving the tourist district. Both

AREA PEDONALE

6,00 - 9,30

San Marco 6

10
11
31 32
67
68

leave from Santa Maria Novella station, but line A crosses the centre, from the Duomo to the Piazza Beccaria by way of Santa Croce, and line D serves l'Oltr'Arno, from the Ponte Vecchio to the San Niccoló Gate, via the Palazzo Pitti and Santo Spirito. Line C, on the other hand, runs alongside the Lungarno to the Piazza Piave (near Santa Croce).

a lot of journeys in the course of a day, it's better to buy a ticket valid for three hours (L2,500) or 24 hours (L6,000). However, you must have a ticket before getting on the bus and stamp it as soon as you get on. And remember, you can always buy a ticket from the driver in an emergency, even if it means paying a 100% surcharge.

The other lines that will be useful to you during your stay are bus 7, which goes to Fiesole, bus 10, which goes to Settignano, and buses 12 and 13, which go from the station to the Piazzale Michelangelo and San Miniato. Bus 62 leaves every 25 minutes from the station for Amerigo Vespucci Airport. Bus 70 is a night bus that runs from the station to Campo di Marte. Most buses run from 6am to 11pm on weekdays, while lines A and D run from 7am to 8pm every day. Single tickets are on sale at tobacconists', newsagents' and Ataf ticket offices. There are only a few ticket machines outside the station. Single tickets (L1,500) are valid for an hour, however many buses you get on. If you expect to make

BY TAXI
Only take the official white taxis with a 'Taxi' sign on the roof. They're identified by the name of an Italian town and a number you'll

be told if you book by phone. Always check the cost of a pick-up (L4,300 in the daytime, L9,300 from 10pm to 6am, and L7,300 on Sundays) and remember you'll be asked to pay a supplement of L1,000 per item of luggage and

L3,000 for a radio taxi. Expect to pay L10,000-15,000 for a journey in the city and L25,000-30,000 to go to the airport. Bear in mind also that it will cost far more if you're picked up at the airport.

Radio Taxi
☎ 055 42 42, 47 98, 43 90.

MAKING A PHONE CALL

All Italians seem to walk around with their moblie phones glued to their ears, but if, unlike the Italians, you haven't got a *telefonino* or *handyphone*, (mobile phone), you won't have any trouble finding an orange public telephone. These operate using units (*scatti*) that you pay for at the cash desk, coins (100, 200 and 500 lire) and phone cards (remember to break the corner before using one). Cards are on sale at tobacconists', newsagents' and telecom offices for 5,000, 10,000 and 15,000 lire. For long calls abroad, there are also 12,000, 25,000, 50,000 and 100,000 lire cards. There are even public telephones that take *Pubblifax* cards that allow you to send faxes.

If you'd rather phone from the comfort of your hotel, bear in mind that the calls will be charged at much higher rates. If you have an international telephone charge card with an access number, you can usually use these from Italy.

Finally, if you want to make a local call, simply dial the 6 or 7 digit number, preceded by the code 055. As you see, it's really quite straightforward.

WRITING AND POSTING

You can buy stamps (*francobolli*) as well as single envelopes from tobacconists' and post offices. If you want something to arrive more quickly, post your mail in the blue letterboxes rather than the more common red ones. The **Central Post Office**, Via Pellicceria, 3 (Piazza della Repubblica), is open from 8.15am to 7pm on weekdays and from 8.30am to 1.30pm on Sundays.

BANKS AND BUREAUX DE CHANGE

Banks are open Monday to Friday from 8.30am to 1.30pm and from 2.30pm to 3.45/4pm. If you want to avoid long queues, go instead to one of the many bureaux de change open every day near the station and Ponte Vecchio.

Using one of the automatic money changers outside the bank isn't necessarily any better and you run the added risk of not getting lire in return or seeing the flap close quickly and irrevocably on your hard-earned cash!

The best place to change cash and traveller's cheques without paying commission is the American Express office, Via Dante Alighieri, 22r ☎ 055 50 981, open. Mon-Fri. 9am-5.30pm and Sat. 9am-12.30pm.

Most banks have cash machines and, in spite of the commission, the exchange rate is better and closer to that charged for traveller's cheques. It's a good idea to change large amounts at a time since a commission is charged for each transaction. Most places of course take international credit cards.

TOURIST INFORMATION OFFICES

This will certainly be the first place you go in Florence to get up-to-date information on the opening times of churches, museums and monuments. 'Permanent' opening times have a nasty habit of changing every three months or so. You'll also need to find out whether any monuments are closed for repairs or refurbishment. Even though the times may change, the staff are friendly and competent, and they'll be able to give you plenty of information about the many exhibitions, concerts and events taking place, as well as bus and train times. Ask, too, for a detailed map of the city, which will be provided free of charge.

APT Via Cavour, 1r
☎ 055 29 08 32/055 29 08 32/3
F 055 27 60 383, 1 Mar.-31 Oct. Mon.-Sat. 8.15am-7.15pm, Sun. 8.15am-1.45pm, 1 Nov.-28 Feb. Mon.-Sat. 8.15am-1.45pm.

APT Piazza Stazione (rotunda outside station near bus stops)
☎ 055 21 22 45, open Mon.-Sat. 8.15am-1.45pm, in summer 8.15am- 7.15pm.

GUIDED TOURS

Since guided tours often consist of unengaging guides trailing forty or so people behind them, the associations of private guides are a better bet. However, if you want to go on a coach tour of the surrounding area (Chianti, Siena and San Gimignano, for example), try

American Express
Via Dante Alighieri, 22r
☎ 055 50 981,
open Mon.-Fri. 9am-5.30pm, Sat. 9am-12.30pm.

Associazione Guide Turistiche Fiorentine
☎ 055 42 20 901.

AGT (Associazione Guide Turistiche della Toscana)
☎ 055 23 02 283.

THEMED TOURS

A better bet are the tours conducted by lecturers and fans of Florence, who will help you discover its hidden charms.

The aim of the **Città Nascolta** association is to make the city's secret places known. The tours are often in English as well as Italian. For information and reservations, ☎ 055 26 38 462.

Florence by bike offers ten themed tours of Florence by bike lasting three hours each and led by a *cicerone fiorentino*. They're another way to see the city, by day or night, through its quiet streets and markets. Sporty visitors can go on day rides in the surrounding countryside. Lazy environmentalists, on the other hand, can go by electric scooter.

Florence by bike
Via della Scala, 12r
☎ 055 26 40 35,
open every day 1 Apr.-31 Oct.
9am-8.30pm.

The Comitato Firenze Promuove (☎ 055 28 84 62) regularly organises theme evenings (Baroque, Renaissance, etc.) including a meal, concert and visit.

OPENING TIMES

Holidays, and therefore weekends to avoid, are 1 January, 6 January, Easter Monday, 25 April, 1 May, 15 August, 1 November, and 8, 25 and 26 December. The large museums are closed on Mondays and open on other days from 8.30/9am to 2pm, except for the Uffizi, Galeria Palatina and Accademia, which stay open until 7pm on weekdays and 10pm in summer. Afternoons can therefore be devoted to visiting the churches, which are generally open from 4pm to 6/7pm. Most shops close from 1.30pm to 3.30pm but stay open until 7/7.30pm. They're closed on Sundays and Monday mornings (or Saturday afternoons in summer). The shops in the main tourist districts generally stay open continously every day of the week.

The Duomo, heart of Florence

The Piazza del Duomo, with its cathedral crowned with a magnificent russet cupola, is an amazing sight. To see this Renaissance image at its best, you need to come early, before the tourists arrive in their droves, or in the evening, when the marble catches the fiery rays of the setting sun. For a truly memorable experience, try combining the sight of the masterpieces around you with the taste of Scudieri's delicious sweets.

❶ Duomo Santa Maria del Fiore★★★

Mon.-Sat. 10am-5pm, Sun. 1-5pm.

Work on the cathedral's dome, started in the late 13th century, finished in 1434 when the stunning ovoid cupola by Brunelleschi was completed. A staircase built between the inner and outer domes affords a close view of this archictectural feat, as well as a panoramic view of the city (entry charge).

❷ Giotto's Campanile ★★

☎ 055 23 02 885
1 Apr.-31 Oct. 9am-6.50pm, 1 Nov.-31 Mar 9am-4.20pm. Entry charge.

Brave visitors who climb the 414 steps to the top of the campanile are rewarded with a marvellous view. Those waiting for them down below have time to admire one of the most beautiful bell towers in Italy. You don't need binoculars to see the 28 marble bas reliefs that illustrate Human Works and Knowledge. The originals are on display in the Duomo museum.

❸ Battistero★★★
Mon.-Sat. 1.30-6.30pm, Sun. and holidays 8.30am-1.30pm. Entry charge.

With its colourful marble and gold mosaics, the baptistery once formed a rich setting for the twice-yearly ceremony during which newborn babies were made citizens of Florence. It's reached via three monumental bronze doors by Andrea Pisano (south) and Ghiberti (north and east). The finest of these is 'The Gates of Paradise' (a replica), four restored panels of which can be seen at the Museo dell'Opera.

❹ Da Scudieri★
Piazza San Giovanni, 19r
☎ 055 21 07 33
Every day except Wed. 7.30am-9pm.

Since the beginning of the twentieth century, these homemade pastries have made life sweet for the most bitter Florentine. *Caffata*, a Florentine speciality made with biscuit and chocolate, can be enjoyed in the little tea-room or taken away.

❻ Museo dell'Opera del Duomo★★
Piazza Duomo, 9
☎ 055 23 02 885
Every day exc. Sun. 9am-7pm (summer) and 9am-6.30pm (winter). Entry charge.

The annexe that is used to store outmoded sculptures and statues has fortunately

been preserved. Models of the cupola seen from different angles illustrate the building of the church, which was only completed in the nineteenth century. Don't miss the *Pietà* by Michelangelo.

❼ Bottega dell'Opera di Santa Maria del Fiore★
Via dello Studio, 23A
Mon.-Thu. 8am-noon, 1-5pm, Fri. 8am-noon.

The *Fabbriceria*, which was founded seven centuries ago to finance the building of the Duomo, is now busier than ever. Like their predecessors, the craftsmen who work here take care of the city's oldest monument, restoring or replacing damaged marble slabs and sculpting marble copies of the original statues, which are now stored away from harmful pollution.

❽ Museo Firenze Com'era★
Via dell'Oriuolo, 24
☎ 055 26 16 545
Open 9am-2pm, Sun. 8am-1pm, closed. Thu. Entry charge.

The former convent of the Oblate Sisters has become the topographical museum of old

❺ CASA DEI TESSUTI★★
Via de Pecori, 20-24r
☎ 055 21 59 61
Every day exc. Mon. am and Sat. pm Jul.-Oct. 9am-1pm, 3.30-7.30pm.

The brothers Romolo and Romano, who are passionately interested in history of fabrics and weaving, will tell you all about the trade that made the Florentines' fortune. The profusion of sumptuous fabrics, many of which were designed by well-known couturiers, is a feast for the eyes.

Florence. A thousand years of the city's history are illustrated here with paintings, engravings, prints and photos. Don't miss the original collection of 14 panels representing Medici villas around Florence.

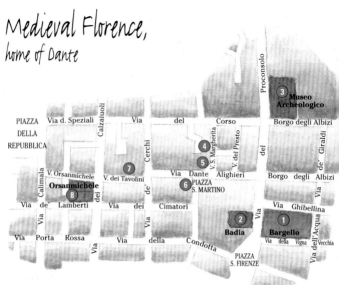

Medieval Florence,
home of Dante

F lorence's austere, grandiose architecture is a reminder of
its turbulent past. The memory of Dante Alighieri, known as the
father of the Italian language, can be seen all around in the maze
of narrow streets that once formed the heart of the wool industry.
This lucrative trade grew up around the Via Calimala and Orsanmichele,
which was a grain store before being converted into a church.

❶ Bargello★★★
**Via del Procosonlo, 4
Every day 8.30am-2pm,
closed 1st and 3rd Sun.
in month and 2nd and
4th Mon. in month.
Entry charge.**

This severe medieval building
that was once the seat of the
Captain of the people is today a
museum of 14th-17th-century
Tuscan sculpture. Around the
sculpture of *Bacchus* by
Michelangelo you can find
works by the great names of
the Renaissance, including
Donatello, Giambologna, and
Cellini, as well as a fine collection of ivories. The Volognana
tower is worth a look.

❷ Badia★★
Entrance Via Dante Alighieri.

This church, in the heart of the
medieval city, has a distinctive
Romano-Gothic bell-tower
and a magnificent carved

wooden ceiling that was added
in the 17th century. Inside is
Mino da Fiesole's masterpiece,
the Tomb of Count Ugo of
Tuscany, and Filippino Lippi's
Madonna and St Bernard.

❸ Museo Nazionale di Anthropologia ed Etnologia★★

Via del Proconsolo, 12
Thu.-Sun. 9.30am-12.30pm, closed Easter Sun. and 1 Nov.
Entry charge.

The former Palazzo Strozzi, which was never completed – hence its name *Nonfinito* – houses one of the richest anthropological collections in Europe. It takes you on a fascinating journey through Asia, Africa, America and Oceania by way of ethnic objects, jewellery and clothes of great beauty.

❺ Dante's House★

Via Santa Margherita, 1
Every day exc. Tue. 10am-6pm.

The author of *The Divine Comedy* (1302), the first work written in the Italian language, is said to have been born in this medieval-looking house. It was, in any case, in the nearby charming little church of Santa Margherita that he saw Beatrice Portinari, his muse and unattainable love, for the first time. He was then just nine years old.

❻ Congregazione dei Buonomini di San Martino★★

Piazza San Martino
Every day except Sun. and holidays 10am-noon, 3-5pm.

A secret place decorated with frescoes from the studio of Ghirlandaio. They depict, with freshness and beauty, the good works done by pious men, who took care of orphans and the sick and distributed bread to plague victims through an opening in the wall.

❼ Cantinetta dei Verrazzano★★

Via dei Tavolini, 18-20r
☎ 055 26 85 90
Every day except Sun. noon-9pm.

As well as Chianti, *grappa* and olive oil from the Verrazzano estate, this friendly wine bar offers delicious local produce served with walnut bread and olives. Make sure you try the canapés with their subtle mixtures of pear and rocket, *pecorino*, honey and bitter orange and wild boar ham – they're really delicious.

❹ SIMONE TADDEI'S WORKSHOP★★

Via S. Margherita, 11
☎ 055 23 98 960
Every day except Sun. 8am-1pm, 3.30-7.30pm, closed Aug.

Bent over his workbench, Simone Taddei makes jewellery boxes from three thicknesses of leather that he polishes with paraffin and a hot iron for a perfect finish. In all, 32 operations, or 20 to 30 days' work, are needed to make one of his delightful caskets or writing cases, which are nevertheless affordable.

❽ Orsanmichele★★★

Via Orsanmichele
Every day 9am-noon, 4-6pm, closed 1st and last Mon. in month.

When the Grain Store, which housed a miraculous

image of the Virgin, was turned into a sanctuary in the 14th century, the corporations turned to the best sculptors of the day to immortalise their patron saints. In this wonderful building, Donatello's calm *St George* vies with Verrochio's fiery *St Thomas* for your attention.

Piazza della Signoria, an appointment with art

The Piazza della Signoria has always been the heart of the city and its administrative centre. With its glorious palace set on one side, it's a favourite meeting-place of tourists and Florentines alike. Concerts are given here in summer and street entertainers perform on fine days, while the people of Florence parade in their Sunday best. The show goes on from dawn to dusk and only stops late at night, leaving the ghostly statues dominating the square.

redecorated for the marriage of Francesco de' Medici. Of interest are the sumptuous apartments where the grand dukes of Tuscany briefly resided.

❶ Piazza della Signoria★★★

The setting for sumptuous festivities and dreadful tortures, the finest square in Florence is peopled with motionless figures. Around Michelangelo's famous *David* you'll find the statues of Judith, the Marzocco, Hercules and Neptune in the middle of his pool. Cosimo de' Medici, seated proudly on his horse, keeps his distance.

❷ Palazzo Vecchio★★
Open 9am-7pm, Sun. 8am-1pm, closed Thu. Entry charge.

The Palazzo Vecchio symbolised the new power of the middle classes. The courtyard was

3 Loggia dei Lanzi★★

Under the elegant *baldachino* backing on to the Uffizi, a row of statues stands guard in place of the imperial lansquenets (*lanzi*), brutal soldiers brought in to restore the power of the Medicis in 1527. Cellini's *Perseus Victorious* and Giambologna's dishevelled *Sabine* are far more preferable to look at.

4 Pineider★
Piazza della Signoria, 13r
☎ **055 28 46 55**
Tue.-Sat. 10am-7.30pm, Mon. 3.30-7.30pm.

This stationer's opposite the Palazzo Vecchio once supplied Napoleon and Lord Byron and owes its fame to its high-quality printing and handmade stationery. The creator of the first leather-cased desk accessories has now extended the range of products to include the indispensable diary, document case and luxury pens. Whether you want something engraved, business cards or even ink to match the colour of your eyes, you'll be spoilt for choice.

6 Galleria d'Arte Moderna Alberto della Ragione★
Piazza della Signoria, 5
☎ **055 28 30 78**
Open. 9am-2pm, Sun. 8am-1pm, closed Tue.
Entry charge.

When you stand next to Marino Marini's horse, you'll have a front-row view of everything that's happening in the square below. If you're interested in modern Italian art, you'll find a fine selection of works assembled by Alberto della Ragione. The years 1930-1945 are the best represented and feature examples of the paintings of De Chirico, Morandi and Guttuso.

8 Uffizi ★★★
In summer Tue.-Sat. 8.30am-10pm, Sun. 8.30am-8pm, in winter Tue.-Sat. 8.30am-7pm, Sun. and hols. 8.30am-2pm, closed Mon.
Entry charge.

We have to thank Francesco de'Medici for having, little by little, turned the offices (*Uffizi*) of the Grand Duchy of Tuscany into an art gallery. This is a grandiose setting for masterpieces by artists such as Botticelli, Uccello, Leonardo

da Vinci, Titian, Caravaggio and Raphael. It all amounts to an introduction to Italian painting. To avoid long hours of queueing, reserve a ticket on ☎ 055 23 47 941. It will only cost you L2,000 more and, since time is precious in Florence, it's well worth the money.

7 Bizzarri★★
Via Condotta, 32r
☎ **055 21 15 80**
Every day except Sat. after. 9am-1pm, 4-7.30pm, closed Aug.

What did the manna in the desert taste like? What colour is dragon's blood? What did the myrrh brought by the Three Wise Men smell like? The answers lie in the mysterious drawers and phials in this shop, which is both a herbalist's and a hardware store. People come from far and wide to buy strange ingredients that are part of age-old recipes.

Borgo Santi Apostoli,
in the shadow of the tower houses

This maze of narrow streets and cul-de-sacs is full of dark passages and towers linked by walkways.
It still seems to ring with the cries of the bloody battles waged by noble families until the dawn of the Renaissance.
It's the Florence of the Guelphs and Ghibellines, a little piece of the Middle Ages dotted with proud palaces and old shops where you'll love to wander.

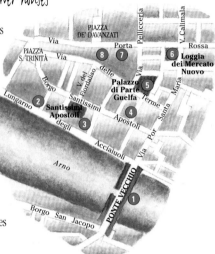

❶ Ponte Vecchio★★★

Weighed down with little shops, where the gold and silversmiths replaced butchers in the 16th century, the oldest bridge in Florence is still as popular a tourist attraction as ever. You can see why Cosimo I had a covered gallery built

above it to allow him to go from the Palazzo Pitti to the Palazzo Vecchio in peace.

❷ Romanelli★★
Lungarno Acciaiuoli, 72-78r
☎ 055 23 96 047
Every day except Mon am in winter and Sat. pm in summer 9am-1pm, 3.30-7pm.

In this unusual gallery, Michelangelo's *Moses* and Donatello's *David* are for sale. Only copies, of course, but executed lifesize, in marble or bronze, and with such skill that your friends will be completely taken in. If your favourite work isn't currently in stock, you'll have to wait three or four months for it to be delivered to your home. Since the cost is counted in millions of lire,

you may prefer to settle for one of the stone boxes instead.

❸ Santi Apostoli★★
Mon.-Sat. 3.30-6.30pm, Sun. and hols. 9.30am-12.30pm.

This little Romanesque church, lost in the tangle of medieval houses, has a fine marble porch opening onto a small square where children

who died before they were christened were buried. Inside, there's a terracotta tabernacle by Della Robbia and flints brought back from the Holy Sepulchre by crusaders. These flints are used to light the sacred fire at Easter during the *Scoppio del Carro* ceremony.

❹ Tassini★★
Borgo Santi Apostoli, 24r
Every day except Mon. am
9am-1pm, 3.30-7.30pm.

Whether you come to have a quick snack or buy Tuscan specialities, you're sure to find the best *antipasti,* hams and cheeses here, as well as a very select choice of wines, *grappa* and olive oils.

❺ Palazzo di Parte Guelfa★
With its fine exterior staircase, this palace is a rare example of the sober architecture that formed a transition between the medieval tower-houses and the imposing patrician residences of the Renaissance.

The façade has a Gothic window adorned with the arms of the captains of the powerful Guelph party.

❻ Loggia di Mercato Nuovo★
The fruit and vegetable merchants have deserted this elegant 16th-century loggia and been replaced by stalls selling souvenirs, scarves and imitation Vuitton bags, all under the placid gaze of *Porcellino*, a bronze statue of a boar

with a much-stroked snout. The Erboristeria del Cinghiale opposite sells original cosmetic products.

❼ Passameneria Valmar★★
Via Porta Rossa, 53r
☎ 055 28 44 93
Tue.-Fri. 9am-7.30pm,
Mon. and Sat. 9am-1pm,
3.30-7.30pm.
Tassels and trimming, ribbons and rosettes, buttons and bows, pendants, piping and pompoms – the art of soft furnishing in all its weird

❽ Palazzo Davanzati★★★
Via Porta Rossa, 13
☎ 055 23 88 610
Tue.-Sun. 9am-2pm.

The antiquarian Elia Volpi, has painstakingly restored this fine medieval residence by means of everyday objects, furniture and tapestries. Inside, you'll be taken back to a different age, when the lord of the manor, Francesco Tommaso Davizzi, had pictures of the legend of the Lady of Vergy painted in his wedding chamber, along with parrots in the dining room.

and wonderful forms in a veritable rainbow of colours to brighten up your home. You'll find hundreds of gift ideas here, too, such as cherubs to hold the tiebacks of your curtains.

From the Santa Trinità to the Repubblica, luxury and palaces

Here you'll pass women dressed in jewels and mink, celebrities and the rich in general.

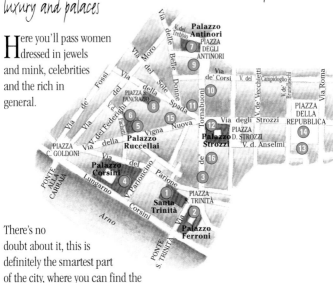

There's no doubt about it, this is definitely the smartest part of the city, where you can find the highest concentration of luxury shops, from high-class jewellers to fashion designers. With its elegant palace façades and unspoilt restaurants, it's the showcase of Florentine good taste.

❶ Santa Trinità★★

Mon.-Sat. 8am-noon, 4-6pm, Sun. 4-6pm.

The whole of the 15th-century aristocracy of Florence is depicted crowded round St Francis and Lorenzo the

Magnificent in the Sassetti chapel. The frescoes by Ghirlandaio provide an unusual way to see the Via de' Tornabuoni and the fashions of the day. Also worth seeing is the *Annunciation* by Lorenzo Monaco, which has pride of place on the altar.

❷ Salvatore Ferragamo: the shoe museum★★

Via de' Tornabuoni, 2
☎ 055 33 60 456
Visits by appointment
Mon. Wed. and Fri.,
closed Aug. and Christmas.

This is the story of Salvatore, a little Neopolitan with a

Salvatore Ferragamo with Audrey Hepburn

passion for fine footwear, who emigrated to California and whose sole aim in life was to make good shoes. He was a very inventive shoemaker who became the darling of Hollywood, where he made shoes for the stars both on and off the screen. These designs can be seen on the 2nd floor of the Palazzo Spini-Ferroni, and his current collections can be found on the ground floor.

❹ Palazzo Corsini★★
Via del Parione, 11
☎ 055 21 89 94
❺ 055 26 81 23
Visits by appointment made two or three days in advance. Telephone on Mon., Wed. or Fri. am, or send a fax to Signora Corsini.

❼ Palazzo and Cantinetta Antinori★★
Via de' Tornabuoni, 3
Mon.-Fri. 12.30-2.30pm, 7-10.30pm.

Since 1506, this elegant 15th-century palace, which stands opposite the only Baroque church in the city, has belonged to the Antinoris, an aristocratic family who own a vineyard renowned for its Chianti. The *cantinetta* where you could once taste their wines has become a trendy restaurant serving authentic Tuscan cuisine at highly undemocratic prices.

❸ Via de' Tornabuoni★★★
This wide avenue lined with majestic palaces has been the most aristocratic street in the city since the 15th century. The wonderful view includes the Ponte Santa Trinità. The *Salotto di Firenze* houses the A-Z of Italian haute couture but, perhaps more interestingly, is home to a number of typically Florentine businesses that have upheld a tradition of quality for several generations.

This palace on the banks of the Arno, with terraces dotted with statues, was built for the illustrious Corsini family and is one of the finest of the Florentine Baroque. A visit to their personal museum allows you to see not only the drawing-rooms but also a very fine collection that includes works by Filippino Lippi, Raphael, Pontormo and other masterpieces unknown to the general public.

fortune in the *oricello* (orchil) trade, a purplish-red dye used by drapers.

❻ I Latini★★
Via dei Pachetti, 6
☎ 055 21 09 16
Closed Mon.
The long queue that forms every evening outside this restaurant, housed in former stables, leaves you in no doubt

❺ Palazzo Rucellai★
Via della Vigna Nuova, 18.

The Palazzo Rucellai's beautiful façade, lined with ornamental columns, has become the epitome of the Renaissance palace. This is hardly surprising since its architect Leon Battista Alberti was passionately interested in Antiquity and may rightly be called a Renaissance man. The Rucellais, who still own the palace, once made a

about the quality of the cuisine. You'll find large parties, as many bottles of Chianti as you can drink, hams hanging from the ceiling and very tempting dishes that are Florentine favourites. In spite of the restaurant's success, the prices are quite reasonable. It's best to come at midday or before 8pm.

8 Museo Marino Marini★★
Piazza S. Pancrazio
Wed.-Mon. 10am-5pm,
Sun. 10am-1pm,
Thu. 10am-11pm 1 Jun-
31 Sep., closed Aug.

The disused church of San Pancrazio is the original setting for an exhibition of works by the sculptor Marino Marini. The *Horseman* placed in the fine light of the apse marks the start of a journey of discovery, or rediscovery, of works ranging from the *Pomonas* to the *Jugglers.* It's a refreshing nod to contemporary art in this Renaissance city.

9 Loretta Caponi★★★
Piazza Antinori, 4r
9am-1pm, 3.30-7.30pm,
closed Mon. am in winter
and Sat. pm in summer.

Since the age of 9, Loretta Caponi has embroidered and sewn with a magic touch, and her daughter Lucia has inherited her passion. The Palazzo Aldobrandini-Rembotti,

with its frescoed ceilings and 18th-century furniture, makes an ideal showcase for collections of fine lace, embroidered linen, delicate christening dresses and other marvellous pieces, which naturally come at a price.

10 Messaggerie Internazionale Seeber★★
Via de' Tornabuoni, 70r
Mon.-Sat. 9am-7.30pm,
closed Sat. pm Jul.-Aug.

The Palazzo Corsi's drawing-rooms with their wonderful painted ceilings are the setting for this very well-stocked bookshop (over 9,000 titles in stock), whose aim is to satisfy an international readership. An important section is reserved for art, and Florentine and Tuscan art in particular. You'll also find new English language publications here.

11 Giacosa★
Via de' Tornabuoni, 83r
Every day except Sun.
9.30am-8.30pm, closed Aug.

Gucci salespeople and mink-clad models sit side by side here in the oldest café in Florence, once reserved for the Antinoris, the Frescobaldis and other aristocrats. It has, however, become a victim of its fame as it only takes a footballer or celebrity to pay a call and the whole place is invaded by muscular bodyguards. The house pastries are delicious, just the same.

12 Palazzo Strozzi★
The ambitions of the banker Filippo Strozzi, who in 1489 had the audacity to build himself a bigger palace than the Medicis', were quickly stifled. After his death in prison in the Fortezza da Basso, his descendants went

to Lyons to make their fortune. This remains one of the most impressive palaces in Florence, with magnificent torchholders that once illuminated the façade during festivals.

⓮ Giubbe Rosse★
Piazza della Repubblica, 13-14r
Every day exc. Wed. 7.30-2am.

In the 19th century, this café-restaurant was a meeting-place of intellectuals, and later, futurists. It still has a cultural side, with literary events on Fridays and Saturdays and exhibitions by contemporary artists throughout the year. The waiters have now shed the famous *giubbe rosse* (red jacket) that gave the place its name, in case you were wondering.

⓮ Piazza della Repubblica★
This vast square, flanked by a pompous triumphal arch and graced by the terraces of the great Gilli and Paszkowski cafés, dates back to the time when Florence dreamed of being the capital of Italy. This ambitious plan swallowed up the old market and ghetto that stood on the site of the Roman forum, as well as dozens of palaces.

⓰ Procacci★★
Via de' Tornabuoni, 64r
☎ 055 21 16 56
Tue.-Sat. 10am-9pm.

Walnut shelves, a green marble bar and round tables all feature in this temple of gastronomy, which opened 110 years ago and has remained unchanged since 1939. All the best people in Florence meet here throughout the day to enjoy the delicious *panini tartufati*, a wild boar pâté or a selection of cheeses washed down with vintage Tuscan wines.

⓯ GIULIACARLA CECCHI ★★★
Via della Vigna Nuova, 40r
☎ 055 21 33 50
Every day except Mon. am in winter and Sat. pm in summer 10am-1.30pm, 3.30-7.30pm.

For 65 years Giuliacarla Cecchi has been at the forefront of fashion. The clouds of organza, knotted silks and plaited ribbons of her creations underline the femininity and personality of her clientele. The wedding, evening and cocktail dresses of your dreams are one-offs designed especially for you. But hurry here as soon as you arrive in Florence if you want your dress to be ready by the time you leave.

The Santa Maria Novella district,

churches and palaces

Two theatrical squares and two sumptuous settings. From the Piazza Santa Maria Novella with its obelisks, once home to the *Calcio dei Cocchi* carriage races, to the Piazza d'Ognissanti, which looks out onto the river, a walk here reveals the timeless elegance of the Florentine aristocracy.

❶ Church of Santa Maria Novella★★★
Sun.-Fri. 7am-12.15pm, 3-6pm, Sat. 7am-noon, 3-5pm.

Behind Alberti's beautiful Renaissance façade lies a Gothic nave lit by stained glass windows decorated by several great Renaissance artists. Don't miss Masaccio's remarkable *Trinity*, the frescoes by Filippino Lippi in the Strozzi chapel and those by Ghirlandaio in the Tornabuoni chapel, as well as the wooden crucifix by Brunelleschi.

❷ Cloister of Santa Maria Novella★★
Open 9am-2pm, Sun. 8am-1pm, closed Fri.

With its cypresses and black and white striped arcades, this is one of the most harmonious cloisters in the city. It contains the extraordinary scenes of the *Flood* painted by Uccello, as well as the Spanish Chapel decorated with frescoes glorifying the Dominican Order. Here, the monks are depicted as black and white sheepdogs guarding the ewes.

❸ Officina Profumo Farmaceutica di Santa Maria Novella★★★
Via della Scala, 16
☎ **055 21 62 76**
Every day except Mon. and Sat. pm Jul.-Aug. 9.30am-7.30pm, free guided tours by appointment.

A long corridor lined with columns leads to a neo-Gothic rotunda filled with the heady perfume of an iris-based pot-pourri. This is the former chapel of the Dominican monks, who passed the secrets of their perfumed essence, balm and ointment making to the Stefani family in 1866. The 18th-century pharmacy, with its collection of stills, old recipe books and Montelupo ceramic pots, and the sacristy (vestry) decorated with frescoes by Mario di Nardo, are the other surprises of this timeless place. You can buy old-fashioned soap and rosewater here.

4 Sostanza★★
Via della Porcellana, 25r
☎ 055 21 26 91
Closed Sun.

This former workers' café, in a small side street, was first opened in 1932 and is still frequented by regulars who come to share the generous meals. *Bistecca alla fiorentina*, tripes and *tortino*, a kind of omelette with artichokes, are served every day, with *baccalà in salsa* (cod) on Fridays. The prices may have gone up since 1932, but the ambience remains the same.

5 Chiesa di Ognissanti★★
Cloister entrance Borgo Ognissanti, 32
Mon. and Thu. 9am-1pm.

This church, given a Baroque makeover in the 17th century, contained the altar and tombstone of the Vespuccis.

It features Ghirlandaio's painting of the famous navigator Amerigo Vespucci in the company of Simonetta, Guiliano de' Medici's mistress. Don't miss Botticelli's painting of St Augustine or the *Last Supper* painted in the old refectory that is said to have inspired Leonardo da Vinci.

6 Hotel Excelsior★★★
Piazza Ognissanti, 3
☎ 055 26 42 01.

Stop for a coffee in the Art Deco setting of the Donatello bar and visit – even if you don't stay at – the smartest hotel in Florence. This restored 16th-century palace and the neighbouring 13th-century mansion that became its annexe in 1925, are decorated throughout with brocades, tapestries, multicoloured marble and antiques. This place is the height of aristocratic refinement.

8 VIA DE' FOSSI★

The Via de' Fossi is a street full of antique dealers and unusual shops, such as **Lisio Tessuti d'Arte** (no. 45r). Here, you'll be able to find a historical costume if you want to take part in the Calcio, as well as reproductions of old fabrics.

7 Palazzo Lenzi-Quaratesi★

Since 1909, this 15th-century palace has housed the French Institute of Florence, which stages exhibitions by French artists, seasons of French films and operatic concerts which are held in a beautiful room decorated with frescoes. It also contains the offices of the French Consulate. There's even a French bookshop on the ground floor.

The San Lorenzo district, the Medici stronghold

H ere, more than anywhere else, the Medicis have left behind constant reminders of their activities as humanist patrons. From their parish church overlooking the Piazza

(map with labels:)

Via Cavour
Via Pier Antonio Micheli
Chiostro dello Scalzo 7
V. della Dogana La
Giardino 8 **dei Semplici**
V. 27 Aprile
Via del Gallo
Via degli Arazzieri
San Marco 6
Cenacolo di Sant'Apollonia 5
V. S. Reparata
Via Panicale
PIAZZA SAN MARCO
Via S. Orsola
Via Taddea
Via Rosina
Guella
Ricasoli
V. degli Alfani
Mercato Centrale 4
Via dell' Ariento
PIAZZA DEL MERCATO CENTRALE
Via della Stufa
Via de' Ginori
Via
Cappelle Medicee 3
Borgo la Noce
San Lorenzo 2
Palazzo Medici-Riccardi 1
PIAZZA SAN LORENZO
V. de Gori
Via de' Puci

San Lorenzo, with its cheap market stalls, to the convent of San Marco, where Cosimo the Elder liked to go on retreat, you move constantly from the past to the reality of everyday life.

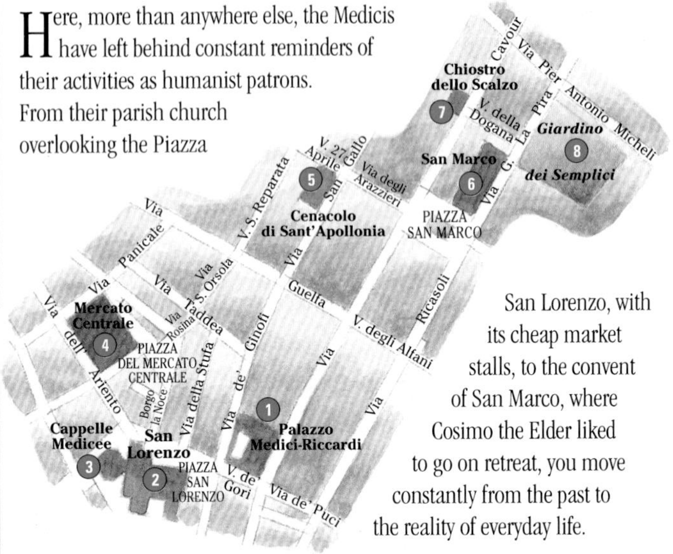

❶ Palazzo Medici-Riccardi★★

Via Cavour, 1
☎ **055 27 60 340 (reservations)**
Chapel tours every 15mins.
9am-1pm, 3-6pm,
Sun. 9am-1pm, closed Wed.
Entry charge.

A palace as modest as its builder, Cosimo the Elder.

In the chapel, the family portrait by Benozzo Gozzoli, showing the young Lorenzo as a Wise Man, conjures up a vision of the East in a Tuscan landscape. It's a real gem. Don't forget to go out and admire the garden too.

❷ San Lorenzo★★★

Every day
7am-noon, 3.30-6pm.

Two great Renaissance masters, Brunelleschi and Donatello, collaborated on this former Medici parish church, on whose pulpits the

latter sculpted one of his major works. Michelangelo, who designed the façade (which was never built), became the founder of Mannerism in the extraordinary vestibule of Lorenzo's library (on the first floor of the cloister, open. Mon.-Sat. 9am-1pm).

❸ Cappelle Medicee★★

**Entrance via the Prince's
Chapel of the church
of San Lorenzo
Open 8.30am-2pm, closed
2nd and 4th Sun. and 1st and
3rd Mon. in month
Entry charge.**

Two minds and two periods
are superimposed on this
mausoleum to the glory of the
Medicis – a luxurious jewel-case
of marble and semi-precious
stones for the grand dukes and
a harmonious chapel designed
by Michelangelo.

❺ Cenacolo
di Sant'Apollonia★★

**Via XXVII Aprile, 1
Every day except Mon.
8.30am-2pm, closed 1st and
3rd Sun. in month. Entry free.**
A discreet entrance leads to
the former refectory of the
Benedictine nuns, where you
can contemplate *The Last
Supper* painted around 1450
by Andrea del Castagno in a
religious silence.

❻ Convento
di San Marco★★★

**Piazza San Marco, 1
Open 8.30am-2pm, closed
1st and 3rd Sun. in month
and 2nd and 4th Mon. in
month. Entry charge.**
Almost all the works of Fra
Angelico are assembled in this
former Dominican convent,
built with the ill-gotten gains
of Cosimo the Elder. At the top
of the staircase leading to the
cells, you're greeted with the
Annunciation.

❼ Chiostro
dello Scalzo★★

**Via Cavour, 69
☎ 055 23 88 604
Mon. and Thu. 9am-1pm.
Entry free.**

Interspersed with ornamental
columns and trompe-l'œil
borders, the superb frescoes

❹ MERCATO CENTRALE★★

**Mon.-Fri. 7am-2pm, Sat. and days preceding
public holidays 7am-2pm, 4-8pm.**

This great steel and glass market hall, built in the 19th
century is the larder of the Florentines, who come here to
stock up on local produce. Try **Nerbone's** speciality, the
bollito, a boiled meat or pig's tripe (*lampredotto*) sandwich.
Other Tuscan specialites, such as *panzanella,* also feature on
the menu, and are all reasonably priced.

painted by Andrea del Sarto
in 1512 depict, with great
simplicity, episodes from the
life of John the Baptist. The
members of this congregation
used to go barefoot (*scalzo*)
during processions.

❽ Giardino
dei Semplici★

**Via Micheli, 3
Mon. and Fri. 9am-noon,
2.30-5pm, Wed. 9am-noon,
Sun. 9am-1pm.
Entry free.**
With the large marble basin
as its focal point, this garden
designed by Tribolo, who was
also responsible for the Boboli
gardens, was originally

planted with strange, unknown
species of plants resembling
16th-century naturalists'
collections. Nowadays, it's a
botanical garden flanked by
an arboretum, perfect for a
walk on a warm day.

Around the Piazza Santissima Annunziata, Renaissance pearls

T his square, surrounded by elegant arcades, is the epitome of Renaissance architecture. In an urban cloister, safe from the hustle and bustle all around, witness the charm of exquisite pictures made from semiprecious stones, fabulous jewels, and admire the triumphant statue of *David*.

❶ Santissima Annunziata★★

Every day
7.30am-12.30pm, 4-6.30pm.

In a little marble temple in a sanctuary built by Michelozzo, the miraculous fresco of the *Annunciation* is preserved. It is particularly venerated by the Florentines. The covered courtyard housing the many *ex votos* has frescoes by Andrea del Sarto and his two brilliant pupils, Pontormo and Rosso Fiorentino.

❷ Spedale degli Innocenti★★★

Piazza Santissima Annunziata, 12
Every day except Wed.
8.30am-2pm. Entry charge.

The delightful babies in swaddling clothes that adorn the loggia hint at the past of this former orphanage.

It was once financed by silk merchants, who assumed responsibility for the upbringing of abandoned children. A picture gallery on the first floor contains works by Botticelli, Ghirlandaio, Piero di Cosimo and Pontormo on the theme of the *Virgin and Child*.

7 Luciano Mario Rossi★★
Via della Colonna, 12-14r
☎ 055 23 40 517
Tue.-Fri. 9.30am-1pm,
3.30-7.30pm or by appt.

This gold and silversmith with a fascination for engraving is a worthy successor to the great stone carvers of the Renaissance. From profiles of Roman emperors carved in agate or violet ruby, to effigies of Cosimo the Elder and small sculptures inspired by the shapes of the gems, all these marvels have modern settings. Allow a month to have the design of your choice made.

3 Galleria dell'Accademia★★
Via Ricasoli, 60
☎ 055 23 88 609
Tue.-Sat. 8.30am-7pm, Sun. 8.30am-2pm, in summer Tue.-Sat. 8.30am-10pm, Sun. 8.30am-8pm
Entry charge.

The centrepiece of the collection of the Galleria dell'Accademia, which was the first academy of painting, sculpture and architecture, is Michelangelo's impressive *David*, whose naked form dominates the gallery. You'll also see extraordinary sketches of slaves by the great sculptor, as well as Palestrina's *Pietà*.

4 Opificio delle Pietre Dure★★★
Via degli Alfani, 78
Tue.-Sat. 9am-2pm.
Entry charge.

The Opificio delle Pietre Dure is one of the most delightful museums in the city. This former factory features landscapes, bouquets of flowers and still lifes made out of semiprecious stones. Stone pictures, table tops and cabinets are born of the virtuoso craftsmen's patient work of cutting and polishing the stones.

5 La Mescita★
Via degli Alfani, 70r
☎ 055 23 96 400
Every day except Sun.
8am-9pm.

Students, workers and local people crowd this tiny bar, which offers not only the traditional glass of red wine straight from the flask, but also a selection of delicious antipasti, pasta and dishes of the day. There aren't many seats but it's worth waiting as it isn't expensive.

6 Museo Archeologico★★
Via della Colonna, 38
Mon.-Sat. 9am-2pm,
2nd and 4th Sun. in month 9am-1pm, closed 2nd and 4th Mon. in month.

Proud of their Etruscan ancestry, the Tuscans from the time of the Medicis onwards have been collecting examples of their wonderful civilisation, including funeral urns and the famous Chimera of Arezzo. Greek art, (including the large François Vase), Roman art and Egyptian art are also well represented in this fascinating museum.

8 Santa Maria Maddalena dei Pazzi★
Borgo Pinti, 58
Every day
9am-noon, 5-7pm
Donation.

You have to cross the church and sacristy (vestry) to get to the former chapter house that still contains a magnificent fresco of the *Crucifixion* by Il Perugino. One of the best works by the Umbrian artist, it was miraculously preserved from the destruction of the convent and the floods of 1966.

Santa Croce, around the markets

Although the dyers and tanners have been asked to go and ply their unpleasant-smelling trades elsewhere, this part of the city still relys mainly on leatherwork in all its forms, from bags to coats. June is the liveliest month, when the historic *Calcio* takes place in the Piazza Santa Croce, but there are plenty of opportunities throughout the year to take in the cheeky humour of the secondhand goods dealers and tradesmen who frequent this working-class district.

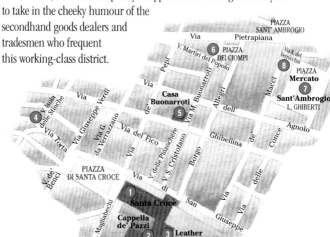

❶ Santa Croce★★★

Piazza Santa Croce
Mon.-Sat. 8am-6.30pm in summer, 8am-noon, 3-6.30pm in winter, Sun. 3-6pm.

A vast Gothic basilica has been erected on the spot where the crowds came to hear the Franciscans preaching.

Michelangelo, Ghiberti, Leonardo Bruni and other famous names of the Renaissance have cenotaphs here, which has earned it the nickname of 'Pantheon of Florence'. A place of pilgrimage for the Romantics, the church has fine frescoes, notably by Giotto, and an *Annunciation* by Donatello.

❷ Cappella de' Pazzi and Museo dell'Opera di Santa Croce★

1 Mar-31 Oct. Thu.-Tue. 10am-12.30pm, 2.30-6.30pm, 1 Nov.-28 Feb. 10am-12.30pm, 3-5pm. Entry charge.

On the south side of the church lies a small secret garden designed by Brunelleschi, the Pazzi chapel, a perfect 14th-century gem, and the cloister with its slender columns. The refectory has been turned into a museum to house works that escaped the flood of 1966. These include Cimabue's *Crucifixion*.

❸ Leather School★★
Piazza Santa Croce, 16/ Via San Giuseppe, 5r
☎ 055 24 45 33
Tue.-Sat. 9.30am-12.30pm, 3.30-6.30pm in winter, Mon.-Sat. 9.30am-6.30pm, Sun. 10.30am-12.30pm, 3-6pm in summer.

In this leather workshop founded by the Franciscans, a dozen master craftsmen have been handing down the skill of leatherworking to their apprentices for fifty years. The tradition is still going strong today. The workshop is the official supplier of office accessories to the King of Morocco and the British Royal Family, and it also produces high-quality bags and small leather articles at affordable prices.

❺ Casa Buonarroti★
Via Ghibellina, 70
Wed.-Mon. 9.30am-1.30pm.
Entry charge.

A visit to the former home of Michelangelo, a Florentine by birth, is mainly of interest for the quality of the drawings and a few terracotta figures that were the first stirrings of his work as a sculptor. Two early works, the *Virgin and Staircase* and *Battle of the Centaurs* show the extent of his repertoire, which was to

fluctuate endlessly between a peaceful serenity and contained tension.

❻ Piazza dei Ciompi★★
Every day
10am-1pm, 4-7.30pm.

In the square and the second-hand shops of the Borgo Allegri, the daily flea market has plenty of items on offer, especially on the last Sunday in the month, when everyone brings the contents of their attics. You won't make many finds except at stand 8, which specialises in travel and sports goods. Try bargaining as the prices displayed are high. You've been warned.

❼ Mercato Sant'Ambrogio★
Piazza Lorenzo Ghiberti
Mon.-Sat. 7am-2pm.

The cheapest food market in the city is held in this rather poor district under a steel and glass roof. The 'show', punctuated by the guttural sounds of Florentine speech, takes place in the square where the stalls of the market gardeners and flower sellers are set up. You can get good, cheap refreshments at one of the *tavola calda* inside.

❽ Caffè Cibrèo★★
Via A. Del Verrochio, 5r
☎ 055 23 45 853
Every day except Mon.
8am-1pm.

Opposite the famous restaurant, you can eat at this little wood-panelled café. The few tables

❹ GELATERIA VIVOLI★★★
Via Isola delle Stinche, 7
☎ 055 29 23 34.
Closed Mon.

The passers-by eating cornets will infallibly lead you to the door of the best ice-cream maker in the city. Winter and summer alike, people queue in front of the counter with its thirty or so unusual flavours that will make you want to come back for more. It goes without saying that it's *produzione propria*.
An institution.

are quickly grabbed at lunchtime and after the cinema, so avoid these times. Come here for a unique menu that changes twice a day, fresh salads and the certainty of finding a very lively, trendy atmosphere with a touch of humour *alla fiorentina*.

Oltrano, the Pitti district

Half way up the slope between the hills of the Boboli gardens and the Arno valley lies the colossal Palazzo Pitti, which takes several hours to visit if you want to see all its countless treasures. All the more reason to enjoy the beauty of the countryside. The scent of the cypresses, the wisteria climbing up the ochre façades and the winding paths in the Boboli gardens all give you the impression of having left the hustle and bustle of the city far behind.

Arno — **PONTE VECCHIO**

Via de' Guicciardini — PIAZZA DI S. FELICITA

Santa Felicità ①

Sdrucciolo de' Pitti ④

Via Maggio ⑤

PIAZZA DE' PITTI — **Appartamenti Monumentali**

PIAZZA S. FELICE — **Palazzo Pitti**

Via Romana ⑧ — ②

⑦ **Galleria Palatina** — ③ **Museo degli Argenti**

La Specola

Viale della Meridiana

Viale dei Platani — Viale di — ⑥ **Giardino** dei Cipressi — **Boboli**

❶ Santa Felicità★★
Open 8am-noon, 3.30-6.30pm.

Preceded by a porch above which runs the corridor that leads from the Palazzo Pitti to the Palazzo Vecchio, this church is the setting for one of Pontormo's most striking works, the *Deposition of the Cross*★★★. Elongated forms draped in acid-coloured robes form a strange group round Christ who is wreathed in an other-worldly light.

❷ Galeria Palatina★★★
Palazzo Pitti
Tue.-Sat. 8.30am-7pm, Sun. 8.30am-2pm, in summer Tue.-Sat. 8.30am-10pm, Sun. 8.30am-8pm. Entry charge.

The Medicis, newly created grand dukes, needed a palace that could house their enormous collection of paintings. This outstanding art gallery, which boasts several masterpieces by Raphael, has as its setting the sumptuous suite of royal apartments whose ceilings are painted with frescoes of mythological subjects.

❸ Museo degli Argenti★★★
Palazzo Pitti
Open 8.30am-2pm, closed 1st and 3rd Mon. and 2nd and 4th Sun. in month. Entry charge.

The Medicis' collection of precious objects is displayed in the grandiose setting of the summer apartments decorated with amazing trompe-l'œil frescoes. The carving of the semiprecious stones and rock crystal is more impressive for its delicacy than the gold and silver plate. Note the antique vases engraved with the name of Lorenzo the Magnificent and the fine collection of cameos.

❹ Giulio Giannini & Figlio★★
Piazza dei Pitti, 36-37r
☎ 055 21 26 21
Every day except Mon. in winter 9am-7pm.

This was the favourite bookbinding workshop of the English at the turn of the century. Giulio Giannini made marvellous photo albums covered in parchment with leather inlays and designs in gold leaf. Fine leather became prohibitively expensive after the war, and he had the idea of covering the books and albums with marbled paper instead. The method is much copied nowadays, though the Gianninis remain the undisputed masters.

❺ Il Caffé★
Piazza dei Pitti, 9
☎ 055 23 96 241
Every day noon-10.30pm.

This café has few tables on a terrace opposite the Palazzo Pitti and more indoors in a fine setting of old walls and fluted columns. Opt for a light lunch (served until 4pm),

tea or even dinner to the strains of blues or jazz. A warm welcome, delicious fresh pasta and no hidden extras await you.

❻ Giardino di Boboli★★★
Entr. in courtyard of Palazzo Pitti or Via Romana, 37
Nov.-Feb. 9am-4.30pm, Mar. and Oct. 9am-5.30pm, Apr., May and Sep. 9am-6.30pm, Jul.-Aug. 9am-7.30pm, closed 1st and last Mon. in month.

A marvellous, naturally-undulating open space stretching away behind the Palazzo Pitti. Tribolo, the landscape artist and designer of the princely festivities, displayed all his talent in the form of box mazes, successive terraces, vanishing perspectives, fountains, statues, fake grottoes and

islands inhabited by gods of the sea. All this as well as a panoramic view of the city.

❼ Museo La Specola★
Via Romana, 17
Every day except Wed. 9am-1pm. Entry charge.

Provided you have a strong stomach, don't hesitate to go and see dissected arms, legs, torsoes and other body parts, as well as the models showing the gruesome effects of the plague on the human body, all made of wax, fortunately, but strikingly realistic nonetheless. See, too, the *Tribuna di Galileo* installed in this former 18th-century observatory.

❽ CANDELE DI FIRENZE★
Via Romana, 30r
☎ 055 23 35 260
Every day exc. Mon. in winter 9am-1pm, 3-7.30pm.

After the anatomical waxes, it's the turn of beeswax, with candles in the shape of Michelangelo's *David*, the *Pietà* and the Leaning Tower of Pisa. Whether it's large altar candles or pretty perfumed candles, this candlemaker certainly doesn't lack imagination.

Santo Spirito, the antiques district

You only have to cross the Arno by the Santa Trinità bridge to escape the hubbub of the city and its crowds of tourists. This is where the major antique dealers set up shop in the nineteenth century to sell off the goods of ruined aristocrats. They work alongside furniture and picture restorers, craftsmen and the young people of Florence, who have adopted the Piazza Santo Spirito as their favourite meeting-place. A very pleasant district, both night and day.

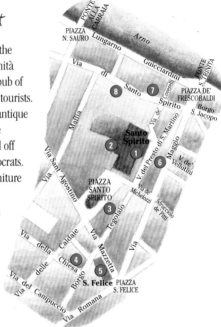

❶ Santo Spirito★★★
Every day except Wed. pm 8am-noon, 4-6pm.

This is one of the finest churches of the Renaissance, a representation of the mathematical harmony conceived by Brunelleschi. The sobriety of the space, the simple rhythm of the columns and the grey *pietra serena*

make it possible to show to advantage the many works of art within.

❷ Cenacolo Santo Spirito★★
Tue.-Sat. 9am-2pm, Sun. 8am-1pm
Entry charge.

To the left of the church stand the convent buildings with their two remaining

cloisters, as well as a refectory containing a very fine *Crucifixion* and fragments of *The Last Supper*, Gothic-style frescoes attributed to Andrea Orcagna. The collector Salvatore Romano displays his collection of medieval statues here.

❸ Caffé Ricchi★
Piazza S. Spirito, 9r
☎ 055 21 58 64
Every day except Sun. 7am-8.30pm (1am in summer).
With the first rays of sunshine, the tables in the square are

occupied by a very mixed clientele, ranging from elegant antique dealers to local craftsmen, who enjoy the fresh salads and pasta served at lunchtime. In the afternoon, old men play cards inside the café and tourists enjoy their ice creams on the terrace. In the evening, the place is taken over by young people.

❹ Legatoria La Carta★★
Via della Chiesa, 10r
☎ 055 29 07 07
Every day except Sat. after.
8am-12.30pm, 2.30-6.30pm,
closed Aug.

You can be certain that the fine marbled paper and leather-bound photo albums you find at Omero Benvenuti's are handmade, since you can see him at work in his workshop which smells of ink, glue and leather. You

may even be lucky enough to be present at the magic moment when the coloured inks in suspension in the marbling vat are absorbed by the paper.

❺ Santa Felice★
This little church founded in the 11th century, is a curious mixture of Gothic and Renaissance, and is worth visiting for its fine frescoes and above all some wonderful Renaissance works by Giotto (such as the crucifix in the choir), Neri di Bicci and the school of Botticelli.

❻ Palazzo di Bianca Cappello★
Via Maggio, 26.

In the Via Maggio, a street lined with majestic palaces that house the best antique dealers in Florence, one façade stands out for its decoration of grisaille frescoes (worked in shades of grey). This was the home of Bianca Cappello, a Venetian beauty with whom Francesco I de' Medici, (who was unfortunately already married), fell madly in love. They later had the privilege of dying together – they were both poisoned!

❼ Il Cantinone★★
Via di S. Spirito, 6r
☎ 055 21 88 98
Closed Mon.

This is a candlelit wine cellar where you'll be doubtless able to improve your knowledge of wine – Chianti in particular and Tuscan wines in general – with the excellent bottles of Montalcino and Montepulciano on offer. Wine tasting is accompanied by good country cooking (*crostini, ribollita, pappa al pomodoro*, wild boar and *bistecca al tartufo*) and bread cooked in a wood-burning oven. The surprise menu with a variety of wines costs L50,000. Ask for more information.

❽ CASTORINA★★★
Via San Spirito, 13-15r
☎ 055 21 28 85
Every day except Mon. am in winter and Sat. pm in summer 9am-1pm, 3.30-7.30pm, closed Aug.

If you're keen on interior design, you'll love this wonderfully Baroque workshop with its turned and carved wood, which is sometimes covered in gold leaf. Here you'll find consoles, frames, fretwork cornices, cherubs, pine cones, Corinthian capitals, and obelisks painted with imitation marble. This workshop, opened by Eugenio Castorina in 1942, is one of the most fascinating in Florence.

Rione San Frediano, the craft district

This is one of the nicest parts of Florence, where the almost deserted streets echo to the sound of hammers, saws, awls and looms coming from dozens of small workshops. Don't hesitate to cross the threshold, you'll always be made welcome by craftsmen, whose skill has been handed down from father to son since the birth of Florence and the arts. Avoid going at the weekend and in August, when everything's shut.

❶ Cappella de' Brancacci★★★
Church of Santa Maria del Carmine
10am-5pm, Sun. 1-5pm, closed Tue.
Entry charge.

Masaccio's contemporaries had already recognised the genius of the painter who founded the Renaissance and was only 23 when he helped Masolino paint frescoes illustrating the life of St Peter. His all-too-human characters, modelled by natural light, stand out against the precious work of his master. The fresco remained unfinished and was honourably completed by Filippino Lippi.

❷ Hemingway★
Piazza Piattellina, 9r
☎ 055 28 47 81
Tue.-Sun. 11am-8pm, closed Jul.-Aug.

In the daytime this is a trendy tearoom specialising in homemade chocolate to drink or eat in the form of cakes and sweets. Later on there are themed evenings, and you can listen to ethnic music as you sip your cocktails and whisky. It's a good place to bear in mind, especially for Sunday brunch, which is served until 2.30pm.

❸ Casa di Bambola★
Borgo San Frediano, 54r·
☎ 055 21 43 67
Tue.-Sun. 10am-7.30pm, Mon. 3.30-7.30pm, closed Aug.

This shop, which seems no bigger than a doll's house, is full of lace and embroidered fabrics stretched over the lampshades. The *lucerna fiorentina*, a lantern that

used to be made of parchment, now comes in an openwork linen version.

4 Stefano Bemer★★

Borgo San Frediano, 143r
☎ 055 21 13 56
**Mon.-Sat. 10am-12.30pm,
4-7.30pm or by appointment,
closed Aug.**

Stefano makes elegant made-to-measure Italian shoes for men only. Once your feet have been measured, you have to wait a month before a pair of hand-stitched shoes is delivered to your home. Subsequent pairs can be ordered simply by sending a sketch of the design. It's undoubtedly expensive, but comfortable shoes really are worth their weight in gold.

5 Corniciaio Pierluigi Franceschi★★

Via San Giovanni, 11
☎ 055 22 06 42
**Mon.-Fri. 8.30am-1pm,
3-7.30pm or by
appointment, closed Aug.**

If you dream of Baroque or Renaissance frames to set off your pictures, go along to the little workshop where this craftsman makes marvels. The choice of 15th-19th century frames is vast and prices vary greatly according to the nature of the work and gilding. Whatever you decide to purchase, it's an investment you won't regret.

6 All'Antico Ristoro di' Cambi★★★

Via Sant'Onofrio, 1r
☎ 055 21 71 34
Open midday and pm, cl. Sun.

Florentines whisper the name of this restaurant to one another, as much for the warmth of the welcome as for the cuisine. The best grilled ribsteak *(bistecca)* in Florence is served here, as well as specialities that can't be found elsewhere, such as *finocchiona*, salami with fennel and fried brains. The wines are exclusively Tuscan, the service impeccable and the prices very reasonable.

8 Brandimarte★★

Via L. Bartolini, 18r
☎ 055 23 93 81
**Mon.-Fri. 9am-12.30pm,
1.30-6pm, closed Aug.**

You'll be welcomed with open arms at this gold and silversmith's workshop where all sorts of objects, from chalices to solid silver salt cellars, are made using traditional methods.

7 ANTICO SETIFICIO FIORENTINO★★★

Via L. Bartolini, 4
☎ 055 21 38 61
**Mon.-Fri. 9am-1pm,
2-5pm, closed Aug.**

Damask, brocade and other sumptuous fabrics are woven on the hand looms installed here when the workshop was founded in 1786. Restored to prominence by the couturier Emilio Pucci in the fifties, the workshop, which isn't open to the public, has a magnificent showroom where you can buy silk by the yard/metre, including *Uccellini* damask (similar to that painted by Benozzo Gozzoli) and *Ermisino*, a shimmering Renaissance taffeta.

The hammering, stamping, engraving, polishing and silver plating are all carried out by specialised craftsmen, justifying the price of these unique objects that are small masterpieces worthy of Cellini. If the workshop is shut, go into the shop at no. 8, which is open on Saturday mornings.

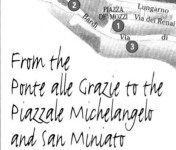

From the Ponte alle Grazie to the Piazzale Michelangelo and San Miniato

As soon as you get to Florence, jump on a 12 or 13 bus and close your eyes until you reach the terminus. Only then, when you see the cupola of the Duomo standing out against the blue-tinged line of the Apennines will you know you've arrived. After you've made a pilgrimage to San Miniato in its fragrant woodland setting, a monumental staircase will take you to the peaceful San Niccoló district stretching alongside the Arno.

❶ Museo Bardini★★

Piazza de' Mozzi,1
Open 9am-2pm,
Sun. 8am-1pm, closed Wed.
Entry charge.

This monumental palace belonging to the late antique dealer Stefano Bardini is an assemblage of doors, fireplaces, ceilings and architectural elements reclaimed from palaces and churches destined for demolition during the building of the Piazza della Repubblica. The drawing room is paved with tombstones, the walls are covered with Persian carpets or embossed leather, and a few fine paintings from the Tuscan Renaissance complete the picture.

❷ Via de' Bardi★★

One of the oldest streets in the city is lined with austere secret gardens and palaces shaded by wide corbelled cornices, like the one where Niccoló da Uzzano, founder of the university of Florence, lived. At no. 14 you'll be met

by delicious aromatic fragrances. This is the home of Lorenzo Villoresi, a master perfumer who sees his clients by appointment (see p. 37).

❹ San Niccoló oltr'Arno★

In the sacristy (vestry) of this charming Renaissance church, a small tabernacle houses a painting by Piero del Pollaiolo, showing the Virgin and St Thomas. The republican Michelangelo found refuge in the bell-ringer's chamber at the foot of the bell-tower when the imperial troops entered the city in 1530.

❺ Antica Mescita San Niccoló★★
Via S. Niccoló, 60r
☎ 055 23 42 836
Closed Sun.

Although the Antica Mescita San Niccoló occupies the thousand-year-old crypt of the neighbouring church, it isn't communion wine that's served here but an excellent Chianti which is accompanied by simple but exquisite cuisine. You can choose from tasty little salads, bean soup and black cabbage, as well as dishes that can't be found anywhere else, such as *peposo*, a speciality of Impruneta, consisting of a meat and wine stew and chilli cooked in the oven. One of the last traditional bistrots, where the atmosphere's always friendly.

❻ Piazzale Michelangelo★★★

In spite of the crowds and tourist coaches, this terrace overlooking the city offers the best view of Florence and the Arno, with the Appenines as a backcloth. Pure magic, especially at sunset or in the early morning mist. A must.

❼ San Salvatore al Monte★

From the Piazza Michelangelo, a cypress-lined staircase leads to this Renaissance church, a favourite of Michelangelo, who nicknamed it 'my country beauty'. The inside is lit by the brilliance of a terracotta by Della Robbia representing a descent from the Cross.

❽ San Miniato al Monte★★★
Open 8am-noon, 2-7pm in summer, 8am-noon, 2.30-6pm in winter.
Sparkling with marble and mosaics on a gold background, the church of San Miniato al Monte can be seen from afar. This little Romanesque gem standing alone on a hill planted with cypresses is as beautiful inside as out, with its zodiacal paving,

❸ ALESSANDRO DARI★★★
Via San Niccoló, 115r
☎ 055 24 47 47
Mon.-Sat.
10am-2pm, 4-7.30pm,
Thu.-Fri. until 11pm.

A gold and silversmith whose designs move between the sacred and profane. He's also cultivated a taste for alchemy and the mysterious — a magic ring to make you invisible, a ring to protect you from the evil eye, or a talisman-pendant containing your lover's astrological stone, as well as fabulous jewellery on the such diverse themes as sin, time and Gothic churches. If you can't afford the same ring as Claudia Schiffer, you're sure to fall for one of these designs.

pillared crypt and raised choir. The monks of the adjacent monastery prepare elixirs based on herbs gathered in the hills according to age old recipes.

Fiesole, a trip to the country

A trip to Fiesole is a perfect way to spend an afternoon. Relax in the shade of the vines, breathe the fresh air of the nearby countryside and sample the local fare. To get here, take a 7 bus from the Piazza della Stazione – the journey will take about half an hour. This refreshing excursion to the hills of Florence will revive you after a stay in the city.

❶ Piazza Mino da Fiesole★★

Curiously built on terraces, the nerve centre of Fiesole was also the old Roman forum. The area is lined with delightful café terraces, and secondhand markets are occasionally held here on Sundays.

❷ Duomo San Remolo★★

To build this Romanesque structure, the ancient city was widely plundered, as is shown by the Roman capitals on the tops of the columns. The works of the sculptor Mino da Fiesole, a local boy and contemporary of Luca Della Robbia, are assembled in Bishop Salutati's chapel. The fine Renaissance triptych (panelled painting) that has pride of place on the main altar is by Bicci di Lorenzo.

❸ San Francesco★
Museum of the Franciscan Missions
In summer 10am-noon, 3-6pm, in winter 10am-noon, 3-5pm.

A short climb rewards you with a fantastic view of Florence in its green setting.

❽ VILLA MEDICI★★
**Via Fra Giovanni
Angelico, 2**
☎ 055 59 417
**Tour of garden by
appoitment with
Signora Mazzini.**

Built in 1458 by
Michelozzo for
Cosimo the Elder, this
was the first Renaissance
villa to have a garden. It
was built in terraces
on a very steep slope,
the first terrace as an

extension of the villa's
loggia, the second lower
down with a pergola and
symmetrical flowerbeds.
To the rear of the villa,
a fountain whispers in
a secret garden. Bought
by the American Lady
Sybil Cutting in 1911,
this was one of Lorenzo
the Magnificent's
favourite places.

You'll be able to rest in the
little Franciscan church that
gives access to the monastery
where the monks have
assembled their souvenirs
of missions to China, the Far
East and Egypt.

❹ **Museo Bandini**★
Via G. Dupré, 1
**Every day except Tue. 10am-
6pm, 10am-7pm in summer.
Entry charge.**

This museum opens onto ten
remarkable terracotta busts
of the apostles that are the
work of an anonymous
16th-century sculptor. It also
features majolicas (tin-glazed
pottery) by Della Robbia.
On the first floor, there's a
fine collection of Tuscan
paintings from the age of
the Renaissance.

❺ **Archeological
site**★★
**Open 9am-6pm,
9am-7pm in summer.
Entry charge, joint ticket
for Antiquarium and
Museo Bandini.**

The Etruscans, and later the
Romans, occupied this
stronghold, which overlooks
the Arno valley and has a
fine 3,000-seat theatre
backing onto the acropolis

and thermae. There's a small
museum that contains
archeological finds made
on the site. The Antiquarium
can be reached by an
underground passage.

❻ **Antiquarium
Costantini**★
Via Portigiani, 9
**Open 9am-6pm
9am-7pm in summer.
Entry charge.**

On the ground floor, you can
see handsome ephebes (young
greek men) frolic on the
ancient Greek vases
from Attica, while the
basement is home to
objects from the
excavation of an
urban district of
Roman times.
A scholarly, educat-
ional exhibition.

❼ **Ristorante
Aurora**★★
Piazza Mino, 39
☎ 055 59 100

A shady, flower-filled terrace
with a marvellous view
and good home cooking
to tempt the appetite –
what more could you ask
for on the day of rest? It's
a good idea to book if you
want a good table, especially
in fine weather.

Rooms and restaurants Practicalities

HOTELS

There are several criteria to bear in mind when choosing a hotel in Florence: the location, star-rating, sound-proofing, view and price. It's by no means easy to find a hotel that meets all these standards yet is still affordable. Staying in Florence is fairly expensive, with prices for double rooms starting at L110,000 in a small family hotel and reaching a staggering L750,000 in a luxury hotel. Our choice of hotels mainly covers small family hotels and small hotels with character, but also includes a few luxury hotels set in historic palaces.

CLASSIFICATION

There are six categories of hotel, from small family hotels to 5-star luxury hotels. In lower-category hotels, the least expensive rooms have showers but no private toilets. From 3-star hotels upwards, the rooms all have the same facilities: direct telephone, television, bathroom with shower or bath and hairdryer. The differences in price are due to the hotels' locations and the services provided. The rates quoted by hotelkeepers (including tax and breakfast) are always the high-season rates, with a reduction of 20% in the low season.

BOOKING

If you're planning to spend a weekend in Florence from March to June, or from September to the end

of October, take the precaution of booking two or three months in advance. All you have to do is send a fax to the hotelier, who will ask you to pay a deposit by postal order or credit card. It's also nearly always possible to book by e-mail as most hotels offer this service. When you book, it's best to specify if you want a single, twin or double-bedded (*matrimoniale*) room. If finding a room seems hopeless, you can always book through a travel agent, though this has the disadvantage of limiting your choice of hotels. About thirty hotels, most of which are 2 or 3-star hotels, are affiliated to the **Family Hotel** organisation
☎ 055 46 20 080
❸ 055 48 22 88,
e-mail topquark.fi@mbox.i.net, www.emmeti.it/topquark, which will find you a reasonably-priced room in a friendly hotel.

RELIGIOUS INSTITUTIONS

You don't have to be devout to seek accommodation in religious institutions, which have the advantage of being quiet as well as cheap (L35,000-50,000 per person). Facilities are basic (no private bathrooms) and the doors close early (at 10 or 11pm). The period from March to June is especially busy because of the number of school parties that flock here.
Suore dello Spirito Santo, Via Nazionale, 8
☎ 055 23 98 202.
Franciscan Missionaries of Maria Santissime Nome di Gesù, Piazza del Carmine, 21
☎ 055 21 38 56.
Oblate Sisters of the Assumption, Borgo Pinti, 15
☎ 055 24 80 583.

TIPS

It isn't usual to leave a tip, except in luxury hotels, where you tip the chambermaid, bellboy and car park attendant.

If the receptionist has been of particular service to you, remember to tip him before you leave. In restaurants, foreigners are expected to leave a 10% tip, though some restaurants add it to the bill automatically. The Florentines, however, aren't in the habit of leaving a tip if the cover charge is already high, especially in *trattorie* (informal restaurants).

RESTAURANTS

Pizzerie specialise in pizzas but also serve pasta. *Trattorie* are convivial, family inns,

where you can eat local dishes. *Ristoranti* are smarter and serve elegant, more refined cuisine. Prices rise as you go from *pizzeria* to restaurant, but the distinction between the two becomes increasingly blurred when certain *trattorie* start charging *ristorante* prices on the pretext of being well known. The long queues that form outside some restaurants are a better indication of the quality of cuisine served inside. Lastly, if you want to eat on the hop, there are plenty of *mescite* and *fiaschetterie* where you can eat *antipasti* and pasta with a glass of Chianti, generally standing up. Along the same lines but a little more expensive and with seating, *cantinette* serve local

cuisine washed down with wines from local estates. Places offering set tourist meals are best avoided. They bear little resemblance to Italian food, which is a pity in a city where they really know how to cook superb dishes.

SET MEALS AND PRICES

A complete set meal consists of five dishes: starters or *antipasti*, *primi* (pasta, risotto or minestrone), *secondi* (meat or fish dishes served without an accompaniment), *contorni* (vegetables, salad and potatoes are listed separately) and, lastly, *dolci* (desserts). Don't worry – even the Italians no longer indulge in such orgies, except possibly on Sundays. You can settle for just two or three courses. On the other hand, don't just order pasta, except at a pizzeria, if you don't want to incur the wrath of the owner. Apart from the larger establishments, very few restaurants offer set meals. However, à la carte meals can be very expensive, with cover and service charges adding considerably to the bill. It's also as well to be aware that the price shown for fish and some meat is per *etto* (100gm/3.5oz). With rib steaks (*bistecca alla fiorentina*)

LAST-MINUTE RESERVATIONS

If you're in Florence and haven't booked a room, don't panic. Go the **ITA** hotel booking centre inside Santa Maria Novella Station. Tell the staff how much you want to pay and where you would like to stay and they'll find you a room. There's no charge for the service.

weighing 600-800gm/ 20-30oz, the bill can come as a nasty shock. Have a look at the menu outside for a rough idea of what you'll have to pay and take special note of the cost of the *coperto*, or cover, (which shouldn't be more than L3,000 in a *trattoria*) and service charge, which should normally only be included in the bill in a *ristorante*. A new generation of restaurant owners opposed to such hidden costs now display yellow *conto trasparente*, (transparent bill) logos, and often even charge a single price for each type of dish. Lastly, to give an idea of price, you can expect to pay L30,000-50,000 for a good meal in a *trattoria* and L70,000-100,000 (or more) in a *ristorante*, not including wine.

Hotels

Duomo

Firenze★★

Piazza Donati, 4
(Via del Corso)
☎ 055 26 83 01
✆ 055 21 23 70
Around L120,000.

In a little square a stone's throw from the Duomo, this old hotel, which has been entirely renovated, is worth considering, as much for its low prices as for its traffic-

free location. The 60 simply-furnished, en-suite rooms all have TV, and the hotel even has lifts.

Piazza della Signoria

Continental★★★★

Lungarno Acciaiuoli, 2
☎ 055 272 62
✆ 055 28 31 39
Around L400,000.

This very comfortable hotel's main attraction is its outstanding location at the entrance to the Ponte Vecchio. The Continental's 48 rooms, decorated in pastel shades, are a subtle mix of old and new. The service is excellent and you'll have a fine view of Florence and the surrounding hills from the sun terrace.

Cavour★★★

Via del Proconsolo, 3
☎ 055 28 24 61
✆ 055 21 89 55
Around L260,000.

The architect and designer Marzio Cecchi accentuated the best aspects of this former palace by blending different periods and styles – Renaissance architecture, Baroque decoration and resolutely contemporary furniture. Very comfortable rooms, a terrace suspended between the Bargello tower and Duomo and excellent cuisine served in the Beatrice restaurant are amongst its other assets.

Santa Trinità

Porta Rossa★★★

Via Porta Rossa, 19
☎ 055 28 75 51
✆ 055 28 21 79
Around L260,000.

This hotel near the Piazza Strozzi, with deep, inviting Chesterfield armchairs and warm light filtering through stained-glass windows, has all the restrained charm of a hotel once frequented by Lord Byron, Stendhal and Balzac, and the Renaissance decor of an aristocratic palace. The 81 rooms are spacious and comfortable, and best of all is the Tower suite.

Tornabuoni Beacci★★★

Via de' Tornabuoni, 3
☎ 055 21 26 45
✆ 055 28 35 94
Around L230,000.

Parquet flooring, antique furniture, Persian carpets, fireplaces and heavy drapes make for a very congenial setting, favoured by ex-President Bush and other famous personalities who, since 1917, have all signed the guest book. Guests are impressed not only by the large, comfortable rooms, all quite different from each other, the high-quality cuisine and the warm welcome, but also by the superb view from the vast flower-filled terrace of this 14th-century palace. You'll need to book at least six months ahead.

Bretagna★★

Lungarno Corsini, 6
☎ 055 28 96 18
F 055 28 96 19
Around L155,000.

On the second floor of the Palazzo Gianfigliazzi, ideally situated on the banks of the river Arno, this very quiet, discreet hotel has 18 simply-furnished rooms (some with a bathroom on the landing), but only one (no. 34) has a view of the Arno. The youngish clientele gathers in the welcoming and friendly lobby.

Santa Maria Novella

Grand Hotel★★★★★

Piazza Ognissanti, 1
☎ 055 28 81 71
F 055 21 74 00
Around L750,000.

In the 19th century this was the most luxurious hotel in Florence, where all the crowned heads stayed, including the Maharajah of Kolapoor, who was cremated in the neighbouring Cascine park. The recent renovation has brought out the sumptuous Belle Époque decor, with its profusion of marble, stuccoes, frescoes, stained-glass windows and Murano chandeliers. The 97 rooms share this refinement, especially the suites hung with

brocade. It costs a lot to stay here, especially if you want a room with a view of the Arno.

Baglioni ★★★★

Piazza Unità Italiana, 6
☎ 055 23 580
F 055 23 58 895
Around L440,000.

A stone's throw from the station, this vast palace, the former residence of the princes Carrega-Bertolini, is a succession of long polished corridors, noble staircases and elegant lounges furnished with antiques. It has 195 beautiful rooms, decorated with frescoes on the 1st floor, and with coffered ceilings on the 2nd and 3rd floors. The vast terrace, with a piano bar offering the finest view of Florence, is the height of refinement. It opens as soon as the weather turns warm.

Aprile★★★

Via della Scala, 6
☎ 055 21 62 37
F 055 28 09 47
Around L240,000.

The frescoes adorning the ceilings of some of the rooms and the lounge indicate that this is a small *Quattrocento* palace converted into a very cosy hotel where guests can feel at home. A delightful garden, where you can have breakfast, and large, comfortable rooms, add to the charm of the place. The rooms at the back have a view of the garden and the bell-tower of Santa Maria Novella.

San Lorenzo

City★★★

Via Sant'Antonino, 18
☎ 055 21 15 43
F 055 29 54 51
Around L250,000.

This hotel is in the heart of a lively working-class district and has 20 sound-proofed rooms equipped with all mod cons. Those overlooking the street are lighter. A very warm welcome and copious breakfast buffet. Special offers are available between 15 July and 5 September.

Santa Croce

Privilege★★★

Lungarno della Zecca Vecchia, 26
☎ 055 24 78 220
❻ 055 24 32 87
Around L260,000.

This hotel in an 18th-century building on the banks of the Arno has been entirely renovated and offers 18 ultra-modern rooms equipped with all services. There's no lift and you'll be torn

between the view of the Arno (with the accompanying noise) and the quiet of the rooms overlooking the gardens.

Santissima Annunziata

Loggiato dei Serviti★★★

Piazza Santissima Annunziata, 3
☎ 055 28 95 92
❻ 055 28 95 95
Around L300,000.

The former house of the Servites, designed by Sangallo the Elder in 1516, closes the elegant perspective of the finest square in Florence. This refinement is echoed in the 30 rooms decorated in simple taste. Heavy Florentine furniture blends with the cream tones, luxurious fabrics, wrought iron and bare stone (*pietra serena*) walls. It's an

excellent place to stay, with fine views, whether you have a room at the front or back. If you come with your family, choose suite no. 12, which is on two levels.

Le Due Fontane★★★

Piazza Santissima Annunziata, 14
☎ 055 21 01 85
❻ 055 29 44 61
Around L260,000.

The main advantage of this ultra-modern hotel, which can be a little on the cold side, is its quiet location in the Piazza Santissima Annunziata. The rooms are certainly comfortable and some even have a jacuzzi. You can hire the hotel Jaguar for effect.

San Marco

Splendor★★★

Via S. Gallo, 30
☎ 055 48 34 27
❻ 055 46 12 76
Around L220,000.

On the 1st floor (no lift) of a 19th-century palace you can find this guesthouse, which has a discreet charm with its old-fashioned furniture and cosy atmosphere. The large rooms overlooking the garden are especially pleasant. After a generous breakfast, you can

bring your own packed lunch to eat in the sun on the flower-filled terrace. Good value for money.

San Frediano

Il Cestello★★★

Piazza di Cestello, 9
☎ 055 28 06 32
❻ 055 28 06 31
Around L180,000.

In a little square opposite the river Arno, a discreet entrance leads up to the 1st floor of this old coaching inn. Converted into a hotel by a charming old couple, it has 10 spacious, flower-filled rooms, facing either the historic river or the sea of red roofs. Rooms 6, 7 and 9, situated under the eaves, are the most attractive. Service worthy of a 4-star hotel for a modest price – a real godsend in Florence!

an elegant courtyard. The high-ceilinged rooms of the old part are the most pleasant, but the hotel is elegantly decorated, snug and comfortable throughout. In summer, you can have lunch on the lime-shaded terrace.

The area around Florence

Villa Natalia★★

Via Bolognese, 106/110
Bus 25 La Pietra
☎ 055 49 07 73
🅕 055 47 07 73
Around L200,000.

Next to the Medici villa, *La Pietra*, perched on a hill overlooking Florence, the delightful 16th-century folly where Queen Natalia of Serbia once resided is a very attractive place to stay. It combines the comfort of large rooms and rustic furniture with the tranquillity of a beautiful Tuscan garden with ponds and statues. Make sure you reserve well in advance. The hotel has a garage.

Liberty★★★

Viale Michelangelo, 40
Bus 13
☎ 055 68 10 581
🅕 055 68 12 595
Around L230,000.

This 19th-century villa, surrounded by a garden is in the residential district overlooking

the city. It is entirely decorated in Art Nouveau style and has a family atmosphere with 17 spacious, comfortable rooms. It's a good place to stay if you like walking or cycling in the countryside.

Bencista★★★

Via Benedetto da Maiano, 4
Bus 7 Fiesole
☎ and 🅕 055 59 163
Around L270,000.

As long as you have your own means of transport, you'll love the tranquillity of this guesthouse, which is surrounded by olive groves at the foot of Fiesole. The large park, fireplaces and old furniture add to the charm of this small, 50-room hotel that has all the qualities a large one, as well as conviviality and a warm welcome.

Villa Aurora★★★★

Piazzetta Mino, 39
Bus 7 Fiesole
☎ 055 59 100
🅕 055 59 587
Around L290,000.

Commanding a superb view of Florence and the surrounding hills, this fine residence, with vine loggias and terraces shaded by vines, is a sure bet if you're looking for comfort, peace and quiet, fine food and a friendly atmosphere.

Pitti

Pensione Annalena★★★

Via Romana, 34
Buses 36 and 37
☎ 055 22 24 02
🅕 055 22 24 03
Around L260,000.

A monumental staircase leads to the 1st floor of this palace ideally situated opposite the Boboli gardens. The 20 large, sunny rooms, are tastefully decorated and offer a refreshing view of the wooded gardens. Ask preferably for a room with a balcony at the back. The excellent buffet breakfast and friendly welcome make it a much-sought-after place to stay. Book ahead.

Silla★★★

Via dei Renai, 5
Buses D and 23
☎ 055 23 42 888
🅕 055 23 41 437
Around L230,000.

The 1st floor of this 15th-century palace at the end of the Ponte alle Grazie is reached via

RESTAURANTS

Piazza della Signoria/ Ponte Vecchio

Le Mossacce★★
Via del Proconsolo, 55r
☎ 055 29 43 61
Closed Sat., Sun. and hols.

A third generation of chefs now stand behind the stoves of this age-old trattoria which serves a traditional cuisine based on good quality local products and fragrant olive oil. Don't miss the *paupiettes* of veal and veal stew (*osso bucco*). Bookings aren't accepted, so be sure to pick a good time to come.

Da Ganino★★
Piazza Cimatori, 4r
☎ 055 21 41 25
Closed Sun.

At Ganino's, film stars, footballers and tourists all sit at the same tables, either inside the restaurant or on the terrace, and share the same bottle of Chianti. The house specialities are fried vegetables, homemade pasta and mushrooms (ceps and white truffles), as well

as the famous cheese tart. A trattoria that's pleasant to visit in summer in spite of the high prices that are the price of its success.

Cammillo★★
Borgo San Jacopo, 57-59r
☎ 055 21 24 27
Closed Wed.

Behind the stoves of this former *fiaschetteria*, Bruno Masiero prepares classical Tuscan dishes with a touch of imagination. His pasta with fresh peas or mushrooms and chestnut flour fritters are especially delicious. The olive oil and wine come from the family estate. Sadly, the prices reflect the restaurant's rather touristy location.

Acqua al 2★★
Via della Vigna Vecchia, 40r
☎ 055 28 41 70.

This highly fashionable restaurant, behind the Bargello, cultivates originality at any price, with its vegetarian dishes, fish with bilberries, chicken with port, and unusual salads as well as holding photo exhibitions. It's better to come after 10pm if you want to see the regular clientele of journalists and actors. Any earlier and it's full of tourists.

San Lorenzo

Zà-Zà★★

Piazza del Mercato Centrale, 26r
☎ 055 21 54 11
Closed Sun.

The trattoria is always packed, so come before or after normal mealtimes to be sure of getting a table. The cuisine is Tuscan, of course, with specialities such as *tagliata* (thinly sliced beef), omelette with cream of tartuffo, and homemade apple tart. The decibel level is high, and the bill is around L35,000-40,000.

Mario★

Via Rosina, 2r
☎ 055 21 85 50
Lunch only
Closed Sun.

People sit elbow to elbow and talk politics, while stallholders chat amongst themselves. It's the best meeting-place in the district, both for the atmosphere and for the very fine cuisine cooked up by Mario's sons. If you like tripe, come on Monday or Thursday. On Wednesday they serve *braciola in salsa*, on Friday fish, and on Saturday *osso bucco*. The bill stays under L20,000, too.

Santa Croce

Il Cibreo★★★

Via dei Macci, 118r
☎ 055 23 41 100
Lunchtime and evening
Closed Sun. and Mon., and 31 Dec-6 Jan., 27 Jul.-5 Sep.

This restaurant near Sant' Ambrogio market has been one of the most popular in Florence for twenty years. Old Tuscan recipes, such as *cibreo*, one of Catherine de' Medici's favourite dishes, are revised in a nouvelle cuisine style and flavoured with herbs. No pasta, but some delicious *minestre*, and specialities of calves' feet, lambs' brains and polenta. The prices are high (around L70,000) but at the neighbouring trattoria of the same name, you can eat the same thing at half the price.

Acquacotta★★

Via dei Pilastri, 51r
(Ciompi)
☎ 055 24 29 07
Closed Sun.

For a change, try the specialities of Maremma, the Tuscan Camargue, beginning with *acquacotta,* a traditional soup made from tomatoes and bread. Grilled dishes, such as thinly sliced beef on a bed of rocket, and classic dishes, such

as *bollito misto* (a mixture of boiled meats), also feature on the menu of this unpretentious little trattoria which has a regular clientele.

Alle Murate★★★

Via Ghibellina, 52-54r
☎ 055 24 06 18
Dinner only
Closed Mon. and Aug.

Designer decor for one of the leading exponents of the new Florentine gastronomy, Umberto Montano. He explores new flavours which can be tried out with his 'taster' menu. Fish features in many of his dishes, which is something rare in Florence. The wine list is impressive and the bill will come toaround L80,000, but much less in the neighbouring *vineria*, which has a more limited choice.

Enoteca Pinchiorri★★★★

Via Ghibellina, 87
☎ 055 24 27 77
Closed Sun., Mon. and Wed. lunchtime, and. Aug.

Molto chic and molto expensive, the classiest restaurant in the city is housed in a 16th-century palace. Tables are set out in the pleasant garden as soon as the weather turns fine. Here you'll find imaginative cuisine and an amazing wine list. Book well in advance and make sure you're suitably dressed.

Santa Trinità

Buca Lapi★★★

Via del Trebbio, 1
☎ 055 21 37 68
Closed Sun. and Mon.
lunchtime.

In the vaulted cellars of the
Palazzo Antinori, the oldest
restaurant in Florence serves
tasty cuisine rooted in the
Tuscan tradition. You have to
taste the *bistecca* cooked on
embers, the *ribollita* and the

onions stuffed with pecorino to
know what we mean. An en-
riching experience (say goodbye
to your diet) for L70,000-80,000.

Oliviero★★★

Via delle Terme, 51r
☎ 055 28 76 43
Evening only, closed Sun.

In an elegant historical setting,
a succession of intimate little
drawing rooms welcomes diners,
while cigar smokers gather in
the piano bar. This is the retreat
of the great chef who revolutionised Italian cuisine in the 80s,
Francesco Altomare. A balanced
menu of fresh meat, fish and
vegetables in season make this
restaurant one of the best places
to eat in Florence, and the wine
list is very interesting, too.

Santa Maria Novella-Ognissanti

La Carabaccia★★

Via Palazzuolo, 190r, bus D
☎ 055 21 47 82
Closed Sun. and
Mon. lunchtime.

Carabaccia is a Florentine
speciality that was introduced

to the French court by
Catherine de' Medici under the
name of onion soup. Onion is,
in fact, the most common
ingredient in the dishes served
by this trattoria, which gets its
inspiration from old recipe
books. Calves' kidneys, wine
stew, vegetable soufflés, oven-
baked tripe and leek puffs – cuisine to discover without delay,
but be sure to book.

Armando★★

Borgo Ognissanti, 140r
Bus D
☎ 055 21 62 19
Closed Tue. evening
and Wed.

This is one of the favourite
restaurants of famous opera
singers, as revealed by the dedi-
cations lining the walls. The
herb-flavoured cuisine is auth-
entically Tuscan, with specialities such as calves' liver with
sage. From the *bruschetta* to the
dessert, everything is delicious
and very affordable.

Osteria n° 1★★

Via del Moro, 22, bus A
☎ 055 28 48 97
Closed Sun. and Mon. lunch.

The chef who officiates in the
kitchens of this welcoming
restaurant is Gianni Dante. On
the menu is an assortment of
Italian cuisine and Tuscan specialities, as well as fish fresh
from the market. The set meal
of the day costs L28,000. They
like you to go outside if you want
to smoke.

Osteria del Centopoveri★★

Via Palazzuolo, 31r
☎ 055 21 88 46
Closed Tue., open lunchtime
also Apr.-Oct.

The owners, originally from
Pouilles, give pride of place on
the menu to fish and seafood
(according to availability),
prepared with great inventive-
ness – mussels with marrow
flowers, prawns with rocket, and
baked fish. Expect well-filled
plates and a great welcome, but
a rather steep bill (L50,000-
60,000). No smoking.

Sabatini★★★★

Via dei Panzani, 41r
☎ 055 21 15 59
Closed Mon.

After a short period of decline,
Florence's grandest restaurant,
which opened at the turn of
the century, has returned to
its former glory, with impeccable
service, an impressive wine list
(500 bottles) and high-quality
Tuscan and international
cuisine. But goodness, it's
expensive!

Pitti

4 Leoni★★

Via dei Vellutini, 1r (Piazza
della Passera)
☎ 055 21 85 62
Closed Wed. Oct.-Easter.

Part rustic and part fashionable,
the decor of this former barn is
in perfect harmony with its creative cuisine, which is much
appreciated by young Florentines
and the people in the worlds of

fashion and film. Hot *antipasti* in winter, salads in summer, careful presentation and a large terrace in a square where cars are seldom seen.

Santo Spirito

Angiolino★★

Via S. Spirito, 36r
☎ 055 23 98 976
Closed Mon.

With its check tablecloths, strings of chilli and wheat

and cast-iron stove, this trattoria resembles a castle kitchen. Local craftsman come here at lunchtimes and younger clients in the evenings. The menu includes tastily-prepared vegetables in season and delicious grills.

La Casalinga★★

Via dei Michelozzi, 9r
☎ 055 21 86 24
Closed Mon.

In this restaurant, diners eat informally in a large, neon-lit room with no frills. Delicious home cooking is served by the friendly waiters who aren't short of advice and interesting anecdotes. It's very reasonably priced, so you'll soon become a regular.

San Frediano

Del Carmine★★

Piazza del Carmine, 18r
☎ 055 21 86 01
Closed Sun.

Waiters in bow ties and a few old fogeys on the walls – there's

no doubt about it, this is a traditional trattoria serving decent cuisine at reasonable prices. It has a very wide choice of dishes and a pleasant terrace on the Piazza del Carmine.

Sabatino★

Borgo San Frediano, 39r
☎ 055 28 46 25
Closed Sat. and Sun.

With china decorating the walls, oilcloth-covered tables, hams hanging from the ceiling and bottles of Chianti on the shelves, the scene is set for eating good *casalinga* (home cooking). There is a different set meal every day and a daily speciality, such as *lampredotto* (boiled calves' tripe) on Tuesdays and *baccalà* (salt cod) on Fridays. Inexpensive and delicious.

Vinesio★★

Borgo S. Frediano, 145r
☎ 055 22 34 49
Evenings only, closed Mon.

Marble tables and wooden seats make a simple setting for authentic Pouilles cuisine. It's difficult to choose between the delicious antipasti, fresh pasta and grilled cuttlefish which are accompanied by a choice of a hundred or so different wines from all over Italy. To end the meal, there's a cheese board and choice of desserts. If you like fish, come on Friday or Saturday. Don't worry, the bill won't come as a surprise.

CAFÉS, TEAROOMS AND ICE CREAM PARLOURS

Paszkowski

Piazza della Repubblica, 6
☎ 055 21 02 36
Open 7am-1.30pm,
closed Mon.

PASZKOWSKI
Caffè Concerto

RESTAURANT
PASTICCERIA
GELATERIA

*Piazza della Repubblica, 6
Tel. (055) 21 02 36
FIRENZE*

It isn't so much the panelled restaurant that attracts the crowds, as the large terrace in the Piazza della Repubblica and the concerts that are given there every evening from May to October. You can eat here or simply order an ice cream or coffee. The terrace prices are considerably higher.

Caffè Amerini

Via della Vigna Nuova, 63r
☎ 055 28 49 41
Open 8am-8pm, closed Sun.

For breakfast, lunch or aperitif, choose between *panini, focaccine* and other ultra-fresh snacks in a very chic, secluded setting frequented by the clients and shopkeepers of this most fashionable of districts.

Gilli

Piazza della Repubblica, 39r
☎ 055 21 38 96
Open 7.30am-1pm, 7.30am-9pm in winter, closed Tue.

Those nostalgic for the Florence of yesteryear come to this plush, stuccoed setting to sample the inimitable cocktails named after famous clients, such as Vivaldi and President Bush. Expensively-priced salads and sandwiches are also served, but it's mainly the tea room and terrace that are of interest.

Mai Più Soli

Via San Zanobi, 63
☎ 055 49 99 66
Open 7.30am-11pm,
closed Sun.

You'll never be alone again in the company of the barman and an *Alexandrino*, a delicious coffee topped with a smooth mixture of chocolate cream and chocolate chips. This is where the young people go, and it's also a place where you can stave off

hunger with a tempting pastry or refreshing salad. Happy hour is from 5 to 7pm, Thursday to Saturday.

Il Rifrullo

Via S. Niccoló, 55r
☎ 055 23 42 621
Open 8am-1pm.

To recover your strength after the climb to San Miniato, take a seat in the garden of this friendly café-crêperie which serves a wide variety of fragrant teas and coffees. They also have snacks to nibble on while you read the newspapers which are provided in every language for customers.

Il Triangolo delle Bermude

Via Nazionale, 61r
☎ 055 287490
Open 9am-midnight,
closed Mon.

In this *gelateria*, Vetulio Bondi makes old-fashioned ice cream using fresh milk and eggs. The *stracciatella* with chocolate, *crunk* (chocolate-chip mocha) and *deep chocolate* (chocolate with a liquid chocolate topping) are highly recommended. The *semifreddi*, such as Viennese coffee and lemon with strawberries, are also memorable.

Perseo

Piazza della Signoria, 16r
☎ 055 23 98 316
Open 8am-midnight,
closed Sun.

On the corner of the Via dei Calzaiuoli, this elegant bar-café, where Florentines meet at aperitif time, is renowned for its delicious old-fashioned ice cream. There are around 30 flavours, including *Buontalenti*, which is rich in eggs, and *Pinolata*, to try without delay. In winter you can always settle for a hot chocolate in the nearby café Rivoire.

La Via del Tè

Piazza Ghiberti, 22/23r
☎ 055 23 44 967
Open 10am-2.30pm,
4.30-7.30pm, closed Sun.

An oasis of Chinese, Indian, Japanese, African and Malaysian flavours opposite Sant'Ambrogio market, with nearly 250 kinds of tea to stimulate the tastebuds. A selection of cakes, preserves and delicacies completes a surprisingly varied menu.

Rivoire

Piazza della Signoria
☎ 055 21 44 12
Open Tue.-Sun. 8am-midnight.

The heavenly hot chocolate topped with cream that you sip in a cosy little room isn't all Florence's best-known café has to offer. It also has a vast terrace in the square in which to see and be seen, which justifies the much higher prices charged here. There are tasty *panini tartufati* and delicious pastries, and did you know that an es-

presso drunk at the bar here costs little more than elsewhere?

Carabè

Via Ricasoli, 60r
☎ 055 28 94 76
Open 10am-midnight.

Antonio Lisciandro and Loredana Giuttari have brought the art of making ice cream and sorbets flavoured with pistachios, lemons and walnuts from their native Sicily. The strawberry, mint and lemon sorbets are to die for, and the chocolate ice cream is just divine.

Vivoli

Isola delle Stinche, 7r
☎ 055 29 23 34
Open 7.30am-midnight,
closed Mon.

The best ice-cream maker in the city (see p. 61).

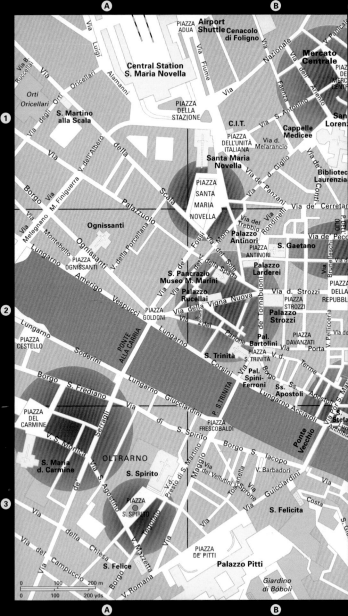

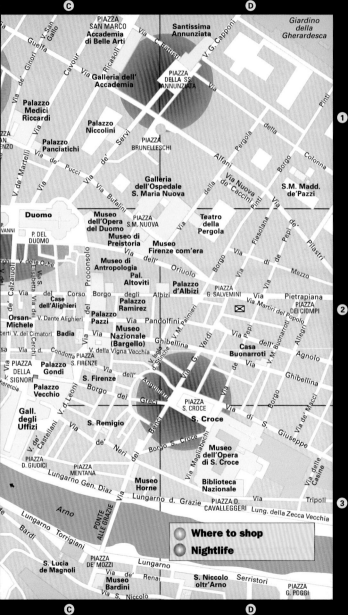

shopping Practicalities

Since the shops are concentrated along the tourist routes, you'll find plenty to tempt you during your stay. Once you've converted hundreds of thousands of lire on the price labels into something more familiar, you'll realise that life in Florence is quite expensive. The best things to buy are Florentine specialities (knitwear, shoes, jewellery, stationery and made-to-measure), which are either less expensive or better quality than at home. And remember not to leave your shopping till Sunday or Monday morning, when most shops are shut.

OPENING TIMES

The shops are generally open from 9.30am to 1.30pm and from 3.30pm to 7.30pm, except on Sundays.

The vast majority of shops close on Monday mornings or Saturday afternoons from June to September. Only the shops in the busiest tourist districts are allowed to stay open continuously every day, including Sunday. August is the month when people traditionally take their holidays. Shops close for at least two weeks around 15 August, and some for a week between

Christmas and New Year, while craftsmen go on holiday for the whole of August. If there's something you definitely want to buy, take the precaution of phoning before you go to make sure the shop will be open – whatever the opening times on display, it isn't uncommon to find a shop inexplicably shut.

HOW TO PAY

The vast majority of shops take credit cards, especially Visa, Mastercard, Diner's Club, American Express and Eurocard. For the rest, it's best to check the stickers on the door on the way in. Traveller's cheques are accepted in most places, though you may lose out on the exchange rate. You may prefer to use your cash card to withdraw money from a cash machine. Your bank at home will levy a small fee, but the exchange rate is better and it's sometimes easier to pay in cash especially if the shop in question doesn't take credit cards.

WHAT TO PAY

Shopkeepers are obliged by law to display the price of every article and to give you a *ricevuta fiscale* (receipt). Only bric-a-brac traders, antique dealers and jewellers are exempt, and you can negotiate a reduction of around 20% with them if you don't need an invoice. So don't expect to experience the joys of bargaining, except at the Piazza dei Ciompi flea market and the San Lorenzo and Mercato Nuovo markets.

SALES

These are held twice a year, in January and July, from the second week in the month onwards, and are publicised by large signs bearing the words *sconti* or *saldi*. At other times of year, you may see shop fronts entirely masked and displaying a sign reading *vendite*

FINDING YOUR WAY

Next to each address in the Shopping and Nightlife sections we have given its location on the map of Florence on pages 84-85.

promozionali. This is generally a ruse to attract customers, since only a few articles are reduced, while the rest are sold at the full price.

WHERE TO SHOP

The fashion district is found around the Via dei Tornabuoni. The Piazza della Repubblica, Via Roma and Via dei Calzaiuoli make up another, also fairly chic, shopping centre, with a majority of clothes, shoe and bag shops.

The antique shops are concentrated round the Via de Maggio, while the secondhand dealers have set up shop in the Borgo Allegri, within easy reach of the Piazza dei Ciompi flea market.

The working-class San Lorenzo district, specialising in food, is home to the cheapest shops, while the Santo Spirito and San Frediano districts abound in craft workshops.

SENDING THINGS HOME

It may be easy to send visiting cards or a batch of made-to-measure shirts by post, but the same isn't true of any bulky objects or furniture you buy during your stay. Most shops, especially antique dealers, can send them to you by means of a reliable carrier, who will base his price, including insurance, on the distance and volume in question. Failing this, you

DEPARTMENT STORES

Coin (Via del Corso/Via dei Calzaiuoli) and **Upim** (Piazza della Repubblica) are Florence's two department stores, the latter being the more popular. At Coin, you can find good quality articles, from tableware to clothes, at lower prices than in the other shops. The best place to go for food is **Pegna** (Via dello Studio, 8) a small, luxury supermarket just a stone's throw from the Duomo.

can contact the following carrier:
Ciulli
Via Federighi, 10r
☎ 055 29 20 46.

CUSTOMS FORMALITIES

For citizens of the European Union, there are no customs formalities to complete. You simply have to produce an invoice showing that duty was paid on the goods in Italy. As a rule, you need the authorisation of the Belli Arti, (the Italian National Heritage association), to export objects over fifty years old (especially drawings and paintings), and you may be asked to show the permit and invoice when you go through customs (see p. 8). Beware of buying fake Vuitton or Gucci. If you're caught with a counterfeit article, the item itself and the vehicle transporting it will be confiscated on the spot, and you'll be fined twice the value of the genuine article.

WOMEN'S FASHION

Like Italian women, who spend a large part of their money on clothes, you'll find it hard to resist getting out your credit card. Nothing could be easier in a city swarming with fashionable boutiques offering a wide choice of garments, ranging from expensive, made-to-measure creations to stylish and more affordable ready-to-wear clothes. It will also be a chance for you to buy that designer dress you've been promising yourself a little more cheaply than at home.

Giuliacarla Cecchi

Via della Vigna Nuova, 40r (B2)
☎ 055 21 33 50
Every day 10am-1.30pm, 3.30-7.30pm, closed Mon. am or Sat. pm in summer.

Even if you can't afford the made-to-measure creations of this grand old lady of fashion, go and have a look at the ready-to-wear collection. The fabric and cut are equally stylish, and the clothes have just the same sensuous fluidity, but at a more affordable price, which includes alterations. You'll get a warm welcome, too.

Morbar

Via della Vigna Nuova, 45r (B2)
☎ 055 28 23 02
Every day 10am-1pm, 3.30-7.30pm, closed Mon. am or Sat. pm in summer.

Lace, satin, organdie, taffeta and pearl-embroidered tulle – dream dresses for the bride and all her attendants. Traditional, romantic or a touch whimsical, the dresses are prettily accessorised and made-to-measure in three months, with prices starting at 2.5 million lire. If you're already married, have a look at the ball, evening and cocktail dresses.

Dalfiore

Borgo Ognissanti, 67r (A2)
☎ 055 29 41 32
Every day 10am-1pm, 3.30-7.30pm, closed Mon. am or Sat. pm in summer.

Clara Terreni is the queen of braid and trimming, with which she

edges Chanel-type jackets, sumptuous evening coats and elegant suits. Stunning original designs to wear on dressy evenings out when you get back home.

Basic

Via Porta Rossa, 109-115r (B2)
☎ **055 21 29 95**
Every day 10am-1.30pm, 3-7.30pm, closed Mon. am.

With natural colours and fine fabrics that are crinkled, crumpled or simply draped, and layering that bares the back or shoulders under a modest veil of silk, these beautifully-cut clothes take first prize. From blouses to jackets, there's a huge choice of clothes for young women looking for something original.

Boston Tailor

Via Porta Rossa, 83-85r (B2)
☎ **055 28 79 87**
Every day 9.30am-1pm, 3.30-7.30pm, closed Mon. am or Sat. pm in summer.

The black and white decor sets off fluid, transparent fabrics,

embroidered voile and moiré in sharp, bright colours that flatter the figure. Forget about them unless you're under 35, have a model figure and aren't short of cash. Jackets cost around L440,000, blouses L320,000.

Luisa Spagnoli

Via Calzaiuoli, 34 (C2)
☎ **055 21 38 57**
Mon.-Sat. 9.30am-7.30pm, Sun. 11am-7pm.

A traditional Florentine line for dynamic women who like well-cut suits and fine fabrics. With the accent on knitwear in fairly neutral shades, it's a kind of Italian Rodier. Expect to pay L500,000 at most for a suit.

Luciano Maggi

Via Porta Rossa, 69r (B2)
☎ **055 21 39 97**
Every day 10am-1pm, 3.30-7.30pm, closed Mon. am or Sat. pm in summer.

This young Tuscan designer, who has worked with Armani, designs up-to-the-minute ready-to-wear for daytime or evening, from lamé dresses to suede jackets with mink collars. The ultimate in chic, you can find matching accessories in the same shop. A jacket sells for L380,000, a coat for L2,700,000.

Andrea Sassi

Via Cerretani, 2r (B1)
☎ **055 29 43 23**
Every day 9.30am-7.30pm, closed Mon. am.

A quick look in the window, which is always very attractive, will certainly make you want to come inside this shop belonging to a Florentine designer who specialises in blouses and tops. Alongside these basics, you'll find skirts, trousers and jackets in matching shades at affordable prices, for girls as well as women.

Luisa via Roma

Via Roma, 19-21r (B2)
☎ **055 21 78 26**
Every day 9am-7.30pm, closed Mon. am or Sat. pm in summer.

A sort of hypermarket of avant-garde Italian and foreign fashion

---

ITALIAN SIZES

While you're busy hunting for that snappy little number, bear in mind that clothes sizes in Italy (for both men and women) are different from those at home . Most sales assistants will be able to help you find the perfect fit, but we've compiled easy conversion tables on p. 126 to ensure that the outfit of your dreams not only looks amazing but fits well, too.

displayed on two floors with soul music in the background. You'll find here the extravagant creations of Roberto Cavalli, Rifat Ozbek, Issey Mikaye, Montana, Dries Van Noten, Jean-Paul Gaultier and the rest. The ideal place for women in a hurry, who can dress themselves from head to toe here by moving from one designer to another.

Maçel

Via Guicciardini, 128r (B3)
☎ 055 28 73 55
Every day 9.30am-1.30pm, 3-7.30pm, closed Mon. am or Sat. pm in summer.

A pale wood setting for traditional clothes by GBR in particular, a sub-brand of Armani. Lots of knitwear and pretty prints in basic shades, as well as the fashion colours of the season, jazzed up with fun accessories.

Marcella

Via dei Pecori, 8r (B2)
☎ 055 21 31 62
Every day 10am-1pm, 3.30-7.30pm, closed Mon. am or Sat. pm in summer.

With its white marble decor, this is a favourite shop of Florentine

women, who can find a selection of the best Italian brands here, from lingerie to suits, accessories and sunglasses included. A temple of glamour, perfumed by Lorenzo Villoresi.

Cozzi

Lungarno Corsini, 4r (A2)
☎ 055 21 02 94
Every day 10am-1pm, 3.30-7.30pm, closed Mon. am or Sat. pm in summer.

However conservationists may feel about it, real fur is back with a vengeance. An astrakan-trimmed coat, mink and leopardskin with Texan-style fringes, bouclé sheepskin scarf or more sensible mink-lined raincoat are all Cozzi creations that are guaranteed to turn heads.

Les Copains

Piazza Antinori, 2/3r (B2)
☎ 055 29 29 85
Every day 9am-1pm, 3.30-7.30pm, closed Mon. am.

From jeans to traditional suits and a complete range of matching accessories, this brand aims to dress women aged 20 to 50 for town and country alike. The warm, bright shop has a bar and a small conservatory, as well as a menswear department that will keep your companion happy while you browse and try on clothes.

Sonia Sassi

Via dei Pecori, 7r (B2)
☎ 055 28 06 90
Tue.-Sat. 10am-7.30pm, Mon. 3.30-7.30pm.

For trendy girls, this shop offers crop tops, tight-fitting trousers, leather jackets, cleverly frayed jumpers and shiny fabrics, all at very reasonable prices (trousers L139,000, scarves L39,000).

Prada

Via de' Tornabuoni, 67r (B2)
☎ 055 28 34 39
Tue.-Sat. 10am-7.30pm, Mon. 3-7.30pm.

From very fashionable transparent tops with heavy seams, to long silk dresses and beaded skirts, Prada is the very height of fashion. Young Italians and

as well as an incredible assortment of materials, surprises the most blasé of dressmakers. Romolo, who has very good taste, will help you choose from the various woollens, silks, hand-painted muslins, voiles and crepes, and will show you the fabrics selected by well-known designers at the recent shows. The most difficult thing to do is to stop buying – it's all so tempting.

FASHION ON THE INTERNET

Fashion lovers can now consult thousands of photos of fashion shows on the Internet (www.firstview.com). Only the selections and collections of previous seasons are available free. To find out more, you'll have to pay $5.90 an hour.

foreigners alike adore this chic, updated version of seventies fashion. It's a lot to pay for nylon, though, even when it's bags and shoes.

Gucci

Via de' Tornabuoni, 73r (B2)
☎ 055 26 40 11
Every day 10am-7.30pm, closed Mon. am.

Another Italian classic, Gucci, offers beautiful clothes in a tasteful setting, where you are served by an army of sales assistants, dressed in black. But super-skinny top models aside, you can't help wondering who could wear these clothes, and you might find that you end up just looking, rather than buying. But browsing is fun, and look out for the classy bags and shoes.

Casa dei Tessuti

Via de'Pecori, 20-24r (B2)
☎ 055 21 59 61
Every day 10am-7pm, closed Mon. am or Sat. pm in summer.

This shop, with an international reputation for top-quality fabrics,

MENSWEAR FROM HEAD TO TOE

These shops are perfect for men who enjoy dressing well. You'll find lots of made-to measure clothes, in a range of fabrics, all with a stylish Italian cut and personalised finishes and details that add that vital touch of elegance. Whether you're looking for a complete outfit or just a shirt, you're entering a world of perfection.

Eredi Chiarini Royal

Via Roma, 16r (B2)
☎ **055 28 44 78**
Every day 9.30am-7.30pm,
closed Mon. am or Sat. pm
in summer.

A very masculine environment spread over three floors of a house decorated with

Persian carpets and crystal chandeliers. The mahogany cupboards and drawers with brass handles contain luxurious clothes that are beautifully cut and finished, such as a sports jacket with suede details and a cashmere collar and

shoes with soles that are rounded to suit your taste and fine silk ties. Top-quality clothes with prices to match, unless you can find your size in the ends-of-range corner.

Eredi Chiarini

Via Roma, 18-20r (B2)
☎ **055 21 55 57**
Every day 9.30am-7.30pm,
closed Mon. am or Sat. pm
in summer.

For 16 to 35-year-olds, a selection of sporty outfits, designer and locally-produced clothes that make use of a variety of materials (rubber belts and stretch-Lycra jackets), trendy cuts and visible heavy seams. This is where you'll have the best chance of finding an emerald-green or

purple shirt to wear with smart jeans, all at more affordable prices than at Royal.

Roberto Biagini

Via Roma, 2/4r (B2)
☎ **055 29 42 53**
Every day 9.30am-7.30pm,
closed Mon. am.

Come here to dress from head to toe in the ready-to-wear or made-to-measure of a Florentine fashion house. There are chiné pullovers and traditional suits cut from beautiful woollen or linen cloth in five or six styles, while shoes can be entirely handmade to order (L400,000 a pair).

Riguccio Mulas

Via Porta Rossa, 10r (B2)
☎ **055 29 34 18**
Every day 9.30am-1.30pm, 3.30-7.30pm, closed Mon. am or Sat. pm in summer.

Up-to-the-minute fashion by Hugo Boss and Kenzo, coordinated with beautiful cotton and linen shirts (Private Lives and A Osé) and elegant Italian knitwear. Clothes for the office or leisure for men who like to dress well and have the means to do so (shirts L99,000-230,000).

Ugolini & Figli

Via Calzaiuoli, 65r (C2)
☎ **055 21 44 39**
Every day 9am-1pm, 3.30-7.30pm, closed Mon. am or Sat. pm in summer.

Having returned in 1966 to the Anglophile style it lost during Hitler's visit of 1938, this 100-year-old shop is the smart man's dressing-room. Cashmere by John Laing, beautiful ties by Filippo Sarri, made-to-measure shirts by Brioni and the Berberi collections for younger men go well with Church's and Cavalli shoes. You can also expect a warm welcome from Signora Ugolini and her son.

Bianzino

Lungarno Acciaiuoli, 32r (B2)
☎ **055 29 34 43**
Every day 9.30am-1pm, 3.30-7.30pm, closed Mon. am or Sat. pm in summer.

This gentleman's outfitter's has been an institution in Florence since 1890. The enormous choice of fabrics (including forty or so different white materials), French seams, tasteful buttons and careful craftsmanship attract a well-heeled clientele. Once your measurements have been taken, and provided you don't put on too much weight, you simply have to place your order and wait a fortnight for delivery of a shirt that will last a lifetime if you change the collar and cuffs. It's a sound investment at L110,000.

Ermenegildo Zegna

Via della Vigna Nuova/Piazza Rucellai 4-7r (B2)
☎ **055 28 30 11**
Every day 9.30am-7pm, closed Mon. am or Sat. pm in summer.

Bruce Willis and John Travolta's favourite designer offers a range of formal clothes and leisurewear combining craftsmanship, elegance and fashion. It's all in the details – buttonholes made with a double thickness of silk

and cotton thread, horn buttons, light, comfortable fabrics, linen and silk ties with geometrical designs, sweater-jackets to wear with jeans or more formal trousers – in other words, the ultimate in modern menswear.

Roxy

Via Cerretani, 33 (B1)
☎ **055 21 50 85**
Every day 10am-1pm, 3.30-7.30pm, closed Mon. am.

At Roxy's, you'll find a wide choice of silk ties and scarves at interesting prices.

CHILDREN'S CLOTHES

If you dream of turning your child into a fashion model with a sailor suit, smocked dress or lace, you'll be spoilt for choice. For more boisterous *bambini*, there's a vast range of sportswear covered in bears, rabbits and Mickey Mouse. They're not exactly the height of fashion, but are guaranteed 100% Italian taste. And you can always take your little darlings back a wooden model of Pinocchio, if you prefer.

Ugo e Carolina
Via Brunelleschi, 20r (B2)
☎ **055 28 78 20**
Every day 9.30am-1pm, 3.30-7.30pm, closed Mon. am.

You'll really fall for the little smocked dresses with puff sleeves, blouses with lace collars, knitted pullovers and bootees with straps and buttons. An embroiderer who once plied her needle for Christian Dior makes the christening robes and layettes, including Moses baskets. Such treasures don't come cheap – an embroidered bib sells for no less than L80,000.

Anichini
Via del Parione, 59r (B2)
☎ **055 28 49 77**
Every day 10am-1.30pm, 3.30-7.30pm, closed Mon. am or Sat. pm in summer.

This small shop devoted entirely to children, sells rather traditional clothes with a touch of imagination. There are pretty prints with matching hats for summer, quilted jackets, honeycomb romper suits, openwork jumpers with cotton collars, sailor suits and headbands embroidered with flowers. There are complete outfits for boys and girls up to 12 years of age, all at attractive prices.

Emilio Coveri
Via della Vigna Nuova, 27-29r (B2)
☎ **055 23 81 769**
Every day 10am-1.30pm, 3.30-7.30pm, closed Mon. am.

Great fashion for smart kids who know what they want. Bright colours, fashionable cuts, practical

Le Civette Kids

Via Porta Rossa 92-95r (B2)
☎ 055 21 41 30
**Every day 9.30am-1pm,
3.30-7.30pm,
closed Mon. am
or Sat. pm in
summer.**

For children aged 3 months to 12 years, this shop has

Zona

Via di S. Spirito, 11(A3)
☎ 055 23 02 272
**Every day 9.30am-1.30pm,
3.30-7.30pm, closed Mon. am.**

Simple, natural materials for the home, as well as for children, who'll love the Pinocchio calendars, cardboard alphabets, moneyboxes made to be broken

materials and amusing prints, such as watermelons and ladybirds. With jumpers at L64,000 and short skirts at L80,000, their mothers won't be ruined financially, and might even find clothes they like in the shop next door, in Via dei Tornabuoni.

B. Del Secco

Via Guicciardini, 20r (A2)
☎ 055 28 28 59
**Mon.-Sat. 9.30am-7.30pm,
Sun. 10.30am-6.30pm.**

Traditional Italian taste – appliqué embroidery, knitted bonnets, coats with velvet collars and matching hats, intricately-knitted jumpers and, for tiny babies, lace-edged bootees, monogrammed bibs and sheets and woollen layettes. A perfect shop for grandmothers who don't feel like sewing or knitting.

practical clothes in colours that never go out of fashion. There's a sporty line, *Superga*, with T-shirts and leggings, and a more old-fashioned *Amore* collection, with Peter Pan collars, pinafore dresses, gingham shorts and embroidered appliqué teddy bears. Expect to pay L70 000-200 000 for an outfit.

into, and china musical boxes. There are also brightly-coloured tin toys for L11,000, and a department selling 100% cotton clothes .

Bartolucci

Via Condotta, 12r (C2)
☎ 055 21 17 73
**Every day 9.30am-1.30pm,
2.30-7.30pm.**

In this former hardware shop, where a life-size carved wooden vintage car has pride of place, you'll find heaps of wooden toys and objects of every size, clockwork or otherwise. They range from a motorbike (L300,000) to a rabbit clock (L60,000) and puzzles (L25,000), not forgetting Pinocchio.

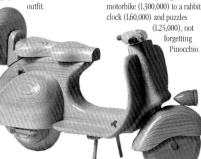

IT'S CHILD'S PLAY

How can you keep your offspring happy while you go on a shopping spree or visit the museums?
Try contacting the following crèches and play centres:
Ludoteca centrale, Piazza Santissima Annunziata, 13
☎ 055 24 78 386
Canadian Island, Via Gioberti, 15
☎ 055 67 75 67
Baby's Club, Via Botticelli, 3
☎ 055 57 65 18.

LEATHER GOODS, BAGS AND ACCESSORIES

Florence is full of small workshops producing high-quality leather goods in limited quantities. Though they're less famous and less expensive than Gucci, who has finally sold his company to the highest bidder, they're nevertheless run by designers who follow fashion closely and use top-quality leather. Remember, a beautiful bag, elegant wallet and kid gloves add a touch of elegance to any outfit.

Braccialini

Via della Vigna Nuova, 30r (B2)
☎ 055 28 84 42
Every day 10am-1.30pm, 3-7.30pm, closed Mon. am.

If you're looking for something slightly unusual, come and see these Indian, oriental and African-inspired designs. There are overstitched patchwork bags in a variety of leathers – embossed, lined, smooth or grainy,

as well as less expensive, washable nylon versions with appliqué work and matching wallets or mules. Expect to pay around L450,000 for a leather bag. Originality is guaranteed.

Bojola

Via dei Rondinelli, 25r (B2)
☎ 055 21 11 55
Every day 9am-7.30pm, closed Mon. am or Sat. pm in sum.

This former wine warehouse has been entirely revamped and displays a vast range of articles on several floors. Ranging from key-rings to cases, they're produced by the leather workshop founded by Felic Bojola in 1892. The workshop's creed is to tan its own hides in order to control their colour and quality, to leave the leather in a natural state with its veining, to produce a perfect finish and to meet the needs of young and old alike. The result is amazing, but it doesn't come cheap.

Furla

Via Tosinghi, 5r (B2)
☎ 055 28 14 16
Mon.-Sat. 9.30am-7.30pm,
Sun. 11am-1.30pm, 2-7.30pm.

Young, trendy bags made of leather or nylon with pure lines and all the accessories –such as

BAGS OF EVERY SHAPE AND SIZE

Whether you stuff everything in it or keep it to essentials, a bag adds the finishing touch to any outfit. A rucksack makes a suit less formal, while a smart bag dresses up an old pair of jeans. Our everyday companion, we need to choose it with care – tall women with figures like models, can carry off any kind of bag, while the shorter, less slimline of us are advised to opt for small bags with short straps rather than large shoulder bags. Lastly, bear in mind that it's not always essential to have a matching bag and shoes!

diaries, key-rings, wallets and belts. The silk scarves and smart plaited metal watches complete a very fashionable range that's within everyone's means. Buy a lined bag, if you can – it'll last much longer.

Il Bisonte

Via del Parione, 11 (B2)
☎ **055 21 19 76**
Every day 9.30am-7pm, closed Mon. am or Sat. pm in summer.

This shop is a treasure trove for the bag hunter. Handbags, rucksacks

and document cases all have a sporty look, with the emphasis on the natural colours of calfskin and strong brass clasps – in other words, tough bags that never go out of fashion, costing L150,000-550,000. One of his latest inventions is an overnight bag made of super-tough fabric normally used for blinds!

Giotti

Piazza Ognissanti, 3-4r (A2)
☎ **055 29 42 65**
Mon.-Sat. 9am-1pm, 3-7.30pm.

Like Gucci, the Giotti family

started out in leather goods with overnight bags, and has remained faithful to its line of canvas and leather luggage, large and small, ever since. When it comes to clothing, on the other hand, there's nothing better than an ultra-light suede jacket with a reversible silk or lambskin lining.

Freon

Via Guicciardini, 45r (B3)
☎ **055 26 44 45**
Every day 9.30am-7.30pm, closed Mon. am or Sat. pm in summer.

A bag to put on the restaurant or hall table that makes the perfect accessory for a little

summer dress or designer suit. Whether it's in the shape of a wheel, a guitar, a heart, a cannonball or a pyramid, it's made of matt or shiny leather and can't be pulled out of shape. These unique bags, which also come in synthetic versions 40% cheaper, are designed by the fertile mind of Istambouliote

Ugolini

Via de' Tornabuoni, 20-22r (B2)
☎ **055 21 66 64**
Every day 9am-1pm, 3.30-7.30pm, closed Mon. am or Sat. pm in summer.

This classy shop is where you'll find the best-quality gloves for men and women. Entirely handmade and super-soft, they're made of peccary, kid, lambskin or wild boar with silk or cashmere

(around L105,000). The pouch bags and silk scarves are just as elegant.

SHOES FOR ALL FEET

Good shoes have always been a source of Italian pride. While other countries have sacrificed individuality to profitability, family businesses that pride themselves on the quality of the leather and finish are of the utmost importance. From classic loafers to fashion shoes, they're all equally supple and just as comfortable for the feet, which can breathe in a leather that's often coloured using natural dyes. Of course, such quality doesn't come cheap, but it's an investment you won't regret.

Cesare Paciotti
Via della Vigna Nuova, 14r (B2)
☎ 055 21 54 71
Every day 10am-1pm, 3.30-7.30pm, closed Mon. am or Sat. pm in summer.

The favourite shoe-shop of Milanese actresses and nouveau-riche Russians is a daring place, with shoes of every shape and kind – square-toed, pointed, turned-up Louix XIV-style, with rubber soles and lizard or snakeskin uppers, strappy sandals and lace-up ankle boots. In other words, ground-breaking designs that will satisfy your every whim. The 'Heroes' collection is just as brilliant at half the price.

Gilardini
Via Cerretani, 8r (B1)
☎ 055 21 24 12
Every day except Mon. am. 9.30am-1pm, 3.30-7.30pm, 9am-7.30pm in summer.

Gilardini is the sole retailer of the Bruno Magli brand of classic, conservative footwear, which is a sound investment for men and women who want to keep their shoes for several seasons. Bear this shop in mind, too, if you're looking for well-made loafers or comfortable shoes at affordable prices (around L180,000).

Tanino Crisci
Via de' Tornabuoni, 43-45r (B2)
☎ 055 21 46 92
Tue.-Sat. 10am-7pm, Mon. 3-7pm.

You can try on the Rolls-Royce of Italian shoes in a cosy drawing room, decorated in velvet and mahogany. The inventor of the

boot with a kangaroo-skin upper and the tube boot that you pull on like a sock, confines himself to the ultra-traditional, and banks on the choice of the leathers and the finishing of the heels and seams, for men's and women's shoes alike. A pair of ladies' shoes costs around L400,000, a pair of men's shoes around L530,000.

Marco Candido

Piazza Duomo, 5r (C2)
☎ **055 21 53 42**
**Every day 9.30am-1.30pm,
3.30-7.30pm, closed Mon. am
or Sat. pm in summer.**

Whether they're fashionable,
eccentric or elegant, Marco
Candido shoes for men and women
come in a combination of fabrics,
including leather and mock
crocodile and a very wide range of
colours to wear from morning to
night. You're partly paying for the
name (L200,000-230,000 a pair).

Casadei

**Via de' Tornabuoni, 33r
(B2)**
☎ **055 28 72 40**
**Every day 9am-1pm, 3.30-
7.30pm, closed Mon. am
or Sat. pm in summer.**

A pure white leather and marble
decor against a background
of *pietra serena* and Roman
columns, underlines the elegance
of these shoes that are both
tasteful and fashionable. With
exquisite court shoes made
of embroidered silk and flat-
heeled city shoes made of supple
leather, there's something for
everyone, provided you can
afford it.

Beltrami

**Via de' Tornabuoni, 48r
(B2)**
☎ **055 28 77 79**
**Every day 9.30am-1pm,
3-7.30pm, closed Mon. am
or Sat. pm in summer.**

A name that has always been
synonymous with quality for
Florentines, has set up shop in a
beautifully-restored Renaissance
palace. While remaining faithful
to the sober, elegant style that won
over the art world, this designer
also has shoes and bags that
appeal to a younger affluent
clientele. Centre-stage, as ever,
is crocodile-skin.

Salvatore Ferragamo

Via de' Tornabuoni, 2 (B2)
☎ **055 33 601**
**Every day 9.30am-7.30pm,
closed Mon. am or Sat. pm
in summer.**

The children of this
shoemaker to the
Hollywood stars
have taken
up the

torch and retained the bow-
trimmed shoe as the house
emblem. Step inside the shop,
if only to admire the ceilings of
the Palazzo Feroni Spini. If you
don't come back out again well
shod, you may at least have
splashed out on a charm bracelet
that's a reminder of some of the
best-known styles.

Mantellassi

**Piazza della Repubblica, 5
(B2)**
☎ **055 28 72 75**
**Every day 9.30am-7.30pm,
closed Mon. am or Sat. pm
in summer.**

From classic, tapered styles
to loafers, by way of pumps
decorated with a little bow, you
can be sure of finding the same
styles here year after year. For
leisurewear, canvas walking boots
may catch your eye, as well as a
few ready-to-wear items that allow
you to complete the conservative
young Italian look.

Fausto Santini

Via Calzaiuoli, 95r (C2)
☎ **055 23 98 536**
**Every day 9.30am-1.30pm,
3.30-7.30pm, closed Mon. am
or Sat. pm in summer.**

A minimalist setting for a display
of the ultimate in chic, avant-garde
footwear. From the flattest of
sandals to
flying
boots,
you'll
find
exclusive
styles for
men and
women to

team up with some really wild
bags. All the prices are around the
L250,000 mark.

JEWELLERY AND GEMSTONES

Y ou're sure to give in to temptation when you see the sparkling shop windows of the Ponte Vecchio, with their cameos, diamonds and amber and coral necklaces. If you're looking for something more original, or for jewellery fit for a queen, here are some jewellers and gold- and silversmiths who design and make unique pieces at a wide range of prices.

Mario Buccellati

Via Tornabuoni, 71r (B2)
☎ 055 23 96 579
Every day 9am-1pm, 3.30-7.30pm, closed Mon. am or Sat. pm in summer.

Since 1929, the delicate designs of a man once called the 'prince of jewellers' have had as their setting a blue-velvet-lined drawing room in the most aristocratic street in Florence. The garlands of engraved gold flowers, traceries of diamonds, brushed silver tassels and opalescent buds are true works of art you can slip on your finger, provided you have a generous partner. Definitely an investment you won't regret.

Settepassi

Via Tornabuoni, 25r (B2)
☎ 055 21 55 06
Every day 10am-1pm, 3-7pm, closed Mon. am or Sat. pm in summer.

A worthy heir to a family who have been craftsmen and goldsmiths since the 16th century, Cesare Settepassi is a renowned gem expert and the largest importer of oriental pearls. This says plenty about the quality of the stones selected for the designs made in his workshop, which is especially well-known for its engagement rings. In association with Tiffany's, the house also offers a range of less expensive designer jewellery, in particular that of Paloma Picasso.

Pomellato

Piazza Antinori, 8-9r (B2)
☎ 055 21 32 00
Every day 9.30am-1.30pm, 3.30-7.30pm, closed Mon. am or Sat. pm in summer.

A magnificent setting with a predominance of dappled grey, the hallmark of this collection of modern, slightly showy jewellery that wealthy Italian women are so mad about. There are enormous cornelians and opals mounted in rings, chunky chains and very stylish steel watches – jewellery to wear if you want to be noticed.

Maggie Maggi

Piazza Pitti, 6r (B3)
☎ 055 29 27 04
Every day 10am-1pm, 3-7pm, closed Mon. am or Sat. pm in summer.

This young gold- and silversmith trained in Florence and perfected her skills in Rajasthan, combining her techniques with her knowledge of Etruscan,

Renaissance and ethnic jewellery to create original designs. These unique and delicate pieces are all entirely handmade and constantly being reinvented. You'll find the prices really interesting, too.

Maria Grazia Cassetti

Via Por Santa Maria, 29r (B3)
☎ **055 23 96 977**
Every day 9.30am-1pm, 3.30-7.30pm, closed Mon. am.

For 20 years, Maria Grazia Cassetti has been designing a line of handmade contemporary jewellery. Her combinations of rubies, diamonds, sapphires and gold are sumptuous creations that can be worn day or night – at a price, of course.

Tharros

Borgo Santi Apostoli, 28r (B2)
☎ **055 28 93 88**
Every day 10am-1pm, 3.30-7.30pm.

Antique jewellery at affordable prices – what a find! OK, they're copies, but with real pearls and stones mounted in silver and gilded copper, all entirely handmade. The Liberty bracelets, Victorian earrings and Art Deco brooches will impress your friends, who won't be able to tell them from the real thing. Prices start at L35,000.

Alessandro Dari

Via San Niccoló, 115r (C3)
☎ **055 24 47 47**
Every day 10am-2pm, 4-7.30pm, Thu.-Fri. until 11pm.

If you're looking for magic rings, jewels representing the seven deadly sins or love charms, this is the place to come (see p. 69).

Luigi Arcuri

Via dell'Agnolo, 61/63r (D2)
☎ **055 23 46 196**
Every day 10am-1pm, 3.30-7.30pm.

This master gem and semi-precious stone cutter also mounts them as exquisite necklaces,

pendants and rings. He may be a little grouchy and only speak Italian, but he's the darling of crowned heads the world over. Your own ideas and designs will be welcome as long as you're not in too much of a hurry.

Torrini

Piazza Duomo, 10r (C2)
☎ **055 28 44 57**
Tue.-Sun. 10am-7pm, Mon. 3-7pm.

This goldsmith's shop has figured in the city registers since 1369. It's the ideal place to buy gold florins identical to those struck for the first time in 1252 and gold medals engraved with the signs of the zodiac or alchemical symbols. A sound investment.

KNITWEAR, SWEATERS AND WOOLLENS

You'll soon see that Benetton, which made Italian knitwear popular the world over, is far from being the best at making sweaters. Alongside their industrial-scale production, there are enormous numbers of independent designers who place the accent on the quality of the wool and cotton used, as well as the finishing, which is often done by hand. Unlike the timeless English styles, the *maglione* is constantly changing with fashion.

Minna Cocchi
Via de' Tornabuoni, 54r (B2)
Every day
10.30am-1pm, 4.30-7.30pm (or by appt.), closed Mon. am.

When she isn't making a jacket on her treadle machine, Minna Cocchi is crocheting or knitting pullovers and scarves. Her highly original one-off designs are a bold combination of colours and materials, such as raffia, that you won't see everywhere you look.

Identità
Via San Spirito, 32r (A3)
☎ 055 29 13 68
Every day 9.30am-1pm, 3-7.30pm, closed Mon. am and 2nd fortnight in Aug.

For Rosario, knitwear is both a passion and a family tradition. At Identità, it comes in extremely simple lines. There are four unisex sizes, sparkling colours as well as the basics, and beautiful materials – a recipe that's all the rage with the young, especially as jumpers sell for L69,000.

John F.
Lungarno Corsini, 2 (B2)
☎ 055 23 98 985
Every day 9am-7.30pm Mar.-Sep., Mon. am and Sun. in winter.

There's nothing like a colourful pattern to brighten up a plain suit. Missoni's famous zigzags appear on all the pullovers, both with sleeves and without, waistcoats, cardigans, shirts and ties. Fairly expensive but very good quality.

Bini Porta Rossa
Via Porta Rossa 72r (B2)
☎ 055 28 90 03
Tue.-Sun. 9.30am-7pm, Mon. 3.30-7pm.

This is the third generation of the Bini family to knit pullovers entirely by hand. Exclusive designs in a variety of stitches, with the emphasis on openwork and airy patterns and high-quality finishing with a crochet hook. It's the right place to come if you're looking for a heavy ribbed pullover or lightweight cardigan to wear under a jacket. Prices range from L100,000-300,000.

Aigue Marine

Borgo Ognissanti, 35r (A2)
☎ **055 29 50 38**
Tue.-Thu. 10.30am-12.30pm,
4.15-7.30pm, Fri.-Sat.
10.30am-7.30pm, Mon.
4.15-7.30pm, closed Aug.

The marvellous knitwear by Michèle Parpaillon, a Frenchwoman who's lived in Italy for 35 years, is sure to get you noticed on the bowling green or golf course. The hand-finished merino wool or cashmere pullovers have leather appliqué embroidery in the form of anchors, horses' heads and golfers. They're very good quality and won't lose their shape. They sell for incredibly low prices, so it's an opportunity not to be missed.

Kent

Via Borgo San Lorenzo, 11r (C1)
☎ **055 28 46 32**
Every day 9.30am-7.30pm in summer, 9.30am-2pm, 3.30-7.30pm in winter.

Kent caters for both sexes, but men benefit when it comes to colour, since they can find Missoni-type pullovers at interesting prices here (L209,000). For women, there are a variety of styles, stitches and textures in wool and viscose mixtures. Prices start at L70,000.

House of Cashmere

Via del Corso, 69r (C2)
☎ **055 23 96 011**
Mon.-Sat.
9.30am-7.30pm.

With cashmere and Shetland sweaters at factory prices (made in Italy but British in style), this is your chance to buy a whole new winter wardrobe. The stock of scarves, shawls, dresses and pullovers is constantly changing, so you're sure to find something you like.

Leoclan

Via del Parione, 11r (B2)
☎ **055 28 32 80**
Every day
9am-1pm, 3.30-7.30pm,
closed Mon. am.

This old-fashioned shop sells beautiful paisley-patterned shawls, wool and cashmere ponchos at L60,000 and wool and silk scarves at L10,000. It's chock-full of bargains, so don't miss out.

WOOL CARE

To keep your favourite woollen clothes looking good for a long time, you need to take care of them. After you've worn a jumper once, air it before putting it away. Always wash woollens in cold or lukewarm water. Wash and rinse at the same temperature or use gradually cooler water for rinsing. Spin drying is generally safe, but for best results, dry the clothes flat.

LINGERIE AND CHIC UNDERWEAR

Whether it's elegant, sporty, delicate or sexy, everyone loves Italian lingerie. Take advantage of your stay in Florence to top up on tights and splash out on a really glamorous lace lingerie set, a naughty corset or a gorgeous embroidered Loretta Caponi silk nightdress. After all, they're often cheaper than at home.

Genni

Via dei Cerretani, 29r (B1)
☎ 055 21 04 13
Every day 9.30am-1pm, 3.30-7.30pm, closed Mon. am or Sat. pm in summer.

The specialist in silk and cotton nightwear, with enough transparency and lace to make sure you don't fall asleep straight away. For when you get up, there are lovely dressing gowns made of comfortable fabrics. All made in Italy and in the best taste.

Nadine

Lungarno Acciaiuoli, 28r (B2)
☎ 055 28 36 66
Every day 9.30am-7.30pm.

Cotton is king here, along with Lycra and microfibre, in combinations of black and white. The lingerie and sportswear by Versace, Dolce & Gabbana and Emporio Armani is designed for athletic men and women They also offer elegant bathrobes and sarongs to match your swimsuit.

La Perla

Via della Vigna Nuova, 17-19r (B2)
☎ 055 21 70 70
Every day 9.30am-1pm, 3.30-7.30pm, closed Mon. am or Sat. pm in summer.

A designer setting for dreamy lingerie and nighties that seem out of reach – but not when you know that the Malizia line is almost as beautiful at half the price. Why shouldn't you splash out on some elegant lingerie from time to time, anyway?

Bisoli

Via Speziali, 12r (C2)
☎ 055 21 13 95
Every day 9am-1pm, 3.30-7.30pm, closed Mon. am or Sat. pm in summer.

An old-fashioned shop where you can get advice along with well-known makes of beautiful Italian lingerie – La Perla, Cotton Club and Gentovivo , as well as gorgeous designer swimsuits. Silk and lace at rock bottom prices (silk knickers L41,000, bra L175,000).

Intimo 3

Via del Corso, 27r (C2)
☎ **055 21 24 15**
**Every day 9.30am-7.30pm,
closed Mon. am.**

Wicked underwear – simple and
frilly for girls, boxer shorts and
one-piece pyjamas for boys.
A selection of reasonably-priced
makes for girls who like baby-
doll and silk pyjamas, with a
vast choice of swimming
costumes in summer.

Emilio Cavallini

**Via della Vigna Nuova,
24r (B2)**
☎ **055 23 82 789**
**Every day 9.30am-1pm,
3.30-7.30pm, closed
Mon. am or Sat. pm
in summer.**

If you want to cover yourself from
head to toe in a patterned or
sequinned body stocking or sheathe
your legs in bright orange, lime
green, leopardskin or sparkling
tights, you can in this unusual shop.
There are hundreds of exclusive
designs in stock, and you are sure
to find something a bit different in
100% nylon or Lycra that will keep
you warm.

American Transfers

Via Nazionale, 123r (C1)
☎ **055 21 82 78**
**Every day 10am-1pm, 3.30-
7.30pm, closed Mon. am.**

The ideal place to live out your
fantasies. There are transparent

plastic slips with giant zip
fasteners, lace-up vinyl
underwear, leatherette suspender
belts, long fake-leopardskin
gloves and shoes with 20cm/8in
heels. Less expensive but just as
much fun are the T-shirts with
outrageous motifs, tattoo
transfers and studded collars.
After all, you only live once . . .

Loretta Caponi

Piazza Antinori, 4r (B2)
☎ **055 21 36 68**
**Every day 9am-1pm,
3.30-7.30pm, closed
Mon. am or Sat. pm
in summer.**

Buy silk nightdresses with
delicate lace and embroidery that
are straight out of a Botticelli
painting (see p. 52).

Quercioli e Lucherini

Via Calimala, 13r (B2)
☎ **055 29 20 35**
**Every day 8.30am-1pm,
3-7.30pm, closed Mon. am
or Sat. pm Jul.-Aug.**

On the wooden counter of this
historic haberdasher's lined
with shelves from floor to
ceiling, Signore Goggioli will
explain all the advantages of the
perennially fashionable Oscalito
underwear made of wool and silk
or lisle and the Ibici tights that
fit like a second skin. If you're
looking for something fancy,
there are vast quantities of
ribbons and rosettes, buttons and
braid, as well as some very pretty
tights at L12,000.

FLORENTINE GASTRONOMY, *DA MANGIARE E DA BERE*

If you cherish the memory of a dish flavoured with white truffles, *cantuccini* dipped in *vin santo* or an outstanding wine, you can repeat the experience at home. All you need to do is take back a few special ingredients and bottles of wine that you'll find without difficulty. Bear in mind, though, that all this shopping adds weight to your luggage, and there are some things that can be enjoyed on the spot.

oils, cheeses and charcuterie – in other words everything that's tempted you during your stay but at more affordable prices than in gourmet grocer's shops.

Pegna

Via dello Studio, 8 (C2)
☎ 055 28 27 01
Mon.-Sat. 9am-1pm, 3.30-7.30pm, closed Wed. pm.

Hidden in an alley behind the Duomo is a small luxury supermarket much frequented by Florentines, where you'll find a wide choice of Tuscan wines,

La Bottega del Brunello

Via Ricasoli, 81r (C1)
☎ 055 23 98 602
Every day 9am-1pm, 3.30-7.30pm, closed Mon.

A little corner of Siena in the heart of Florence where you can taste, if you haven't already done so, the incomparable Brunello di Montalcino, the most expensive wine in Italy, as well as other wines of the

region. It's also renowned for its highly-flavoured olive oil and almond pastries, such as *panforte* and *ricciarelli*.

Pitti Gola e Cantina

Piazza Pitti, 16 (B3)
☎ 055 21 27 04
Every day 10am-1pm, 3-7pm, Sun. 1am-6pm, closed Mon.

This shop sells all the local products, in attractive

bottles – extra-virgin olive oil, balsamic vinegar, grape mustard, mushroom sauce flavoured with white truffles, sun-dried peppers and tomatoes and a fine selection of Tuscan wines that you can taste on the spot. To tell you how to get the most from these ingredients, there are attractive books on Italian cuisine.

Antica Bottigliera del Centro
Via dei Banchi, 55-57r (B1)
☎ **055 29 31 49**
Every day 9am-1pm, 3.30-7.30pm, closed Mon. am.

As its name suggests, this shop sells bottles of every shape and colour – Chianti bottles, Bordeaux bottles (for Brunello),

square-based litre bottles (for extra-virgin olive oil), vinegar bottles and blown-glass demijohns (for grappa). As well as these varied and beautiful bottles, you'll find a vast choice of wines and spirits from all over Italy at very competitive prices.

Zanobini
Via Sant' Antonino, 47r (B1)
☎ **055 23 96 850**
Every day 9am-1pm, 3.30-7.30pm, closed Mon. am.

In a district devoted to gastronomic pleasures, this grocer's shop has one of the best stocks of fresh products (charcuterie, cheese and fresh pasta) and foodstuffs with a long shelf life. Buy naturally-coloured pasta, aromatic oils, *cantucci* and *amaretti* and a few good bottles of Tuscan wine, all at reasonable prices.

Dolci & Dolcezze
Via del Corso, 41r (C2)
☎ **055 28 25 78**
Every day 9.30am-1.30pm, 4.30-7.30pm, closed Sun.-Mon.

Giulio Corti is the big innovator of Florentine patisserie. His selling points are the quality and freshness of his products and a real talent for turning them into delicious desserts. Besides his

famous chocolate cake, you should also try the pear cheesecake, lemon tart and amaretto-flavoured chocolate pudding. To accompany these sweets, there's a delicious Sicilian orange and mandarin liqueur.

Boutique del Cioccolato
Via Maragliano, 12r (off map)
Bus 22, Maragliano 4
☎ **055 36 16 50**
Mon.-Sat. 7am-8pm, Sun. 7am-1pm.

Chocoholics won't hesitate to venture this far to try the specialities of this famous chocolate-maker, who's the only one besides Rivoire to make his own chocolate. You can eat on the spot with a coffee or take away. Amongst the delicious specialities to try are chocolates with cream, orange, vino santo and amaretto fillings, pastries, delicious biscuits or simply bitter chocolate sold by weight.

ANTIQUE DEALERS

There are a hundred and fifty antique dealers in Florence – certainly enough to turn the head of anyone who wants to look for bargains during their stay. Fortunately for your aching feet, they're concentrated in Via Maggio, Via de' Fossi and Borgo Ognissanti. To help you a little in your search for that rare object or item of furniture, we've chosen the largest dealers. After that, it's up to you to choose according to what you're looking for and what you can afford.

Casa d'Aste Pitti

Via Maggio, 15 (B3)
☎ 055 23 96 382
Exhibition Fri.-Sat. 10am-1pm, 3-6.30pm, Sat.-Sun. 10am-1pm, 4-7pm.

After obtaining a personal card that's valid for life, you can attend the auctions held in the palace on Wednesdays and Thursdays. The objects and furniture can be viewed on the three days preceding the sale. If you can't attend the public auction, you can buy the catalogue, which will give you an idea of the Italian market before you do the rounds of the antique dealers.

Giovanni Pratesi

Via Maggio, 18 (B3)
☎ 055 23 96 568
Every day 9.30am-1pm, 3.30-7.30pm, closed Sun. and Aug.

The president of the Association of Italian Antique Dealers has a gallery in a sumptuous palace opposite the Casa de Bianca Capello. He specialises in Baroque and neo-Classical painting and sculpture, of which he possesses priceless examples, and he also deals in beautiful objects (silverware, majolica, porcelain and glass) and furniture.

Guido Bartolozzi

Via Maggio, 11 (B3)
☎ 055 21 56 02
Every day 9am-1pm, 3.30-7.30pm, closed Mon. am or Sat. pm in summer, closed Aug.

In a 16th-century palace bought over a hundred years ago by the antique dealer's grandfather, you will find one of the largest selections of 14th-19th-century furniture, carpets, chandeliers, paintings, sculptures and objects. In fact, everything that can be found in the palaces of the Italian nobility, to which this renowned antique dealer is a frequent visitor. A mine of very rare pieces.

Exporting Antiques

The export of works of art and furniture over 50 year old requires the approval of the Belli Arti (the Italian equivalent of National Heritage), who do appraisals once a week on Wednesdays. The cost of this, including a permit, is L20,000, to which should be added VAT and the cost of transportation and insurance.

Drawings and paintings are very closely examined, though a Giotto recently managed to slip through the net. A good antique dealer will tell you all about these formalities before any major purchase. For more run-of-the-mill objects that are smaller and less valuable, a permit isn't absolutely essential. The invoice, on the other hand, is. You may be asked to produce it when you go through customs, and it will be useful if you ever want to sell your purchase or if you're burgled and need to fill in an insurance claim form.

Bruno Gallori-Turchi

Via Maggio, 14r (B3)
☎ 055 28 22 79
Every day 9.30am-1pm, 3.30-7.30pm, closed Mon. am or Sat. pm Jun.-Sep.

This is the perfect place for anyone interested in old weaponry, especially armour and swords. This antique dealer is also passionately interested in 16th-18th-century bronze objects, porcelain and majolica from all over Italy.

Antica Libreria Antiquaria

Via Ricasoli, 14r (C1)
☎ 055 21 68 35
Every day 9am-1pm, 4-7.30pm, closed Mon. in winter and Sat. in summer.

With its precious wooden shelves and gilded pilasters, this fine bookshop, one of the oldest in Italy, forms a magnificent setting for leather-bound, early printed books and manuscripts. The shop is rich in old histories of Florence and Tuscany, and also has a large number of rare books in various languages, as well as drawings and engravings from different periods.

Galleria Lapiccirella

Borgo Ognissanti, 54-56r (A2)
☎ 055 28 49 02
Every day 9.30am-1pm, 3.30-7.30pm, closed Mon. am or Sat. pm in summer.

You'll think you're entering the drawing room of an interior designer, with a neo-Classical marble bust on an Empire console, mirrors with gilded wooden frames, huge dark red velvet cardinal's chairs, an 18th-century portrait, bronzes and curiosities – a beautiful setting that can help you picture the 16th to 19th-century furniture in your own home, even if it's modern.

Bellini & Figli

Lungarno Soderini, 5 (A2)
☎ 055 21 40 31
Mon.-Fri. 9am-1pm, 4-7.30pm.

A beautiful patrician residence on the banks of the Arno furnished with high-quality objects and pictures.

Cassetti

Ponte Vecchio, 52r (B3)
☎ 055 23 96 028
Tue.-Sat. 9am-7.30pm, Nov., Jan. and Feb. 9.30am-1pm, 3.30-7.30pm, closed Sun.-Mon.

If you like old jewellery, Signora Cassetti, who comes from an old family of goldsmiths, has the finest pieces by Tiffany, Van Cleef and Cartier, as well as a large collection of David Webbs. In her tiny *bottega* on the Ponte Vecchio, Victorian diamond necklaces, emeralds, Art Deco jewellery and cascades of pearls are displayed on black velvet. Must be seen.

TERRACOTTA, MAJOLICA AND CERAMICS

Whether they're glazed, patterned with fruit and flowers or simply the rich red colour of the earth, Tuscan ceramics are very decorative in both house and garden. Prices vary greatly according to whether you're interested in buying everyday tableware, a reproduction of a piece of old majolica, or even an antique. For any important purchase, insist on a certificate of authenticity, and beware of cheap majolica, which is made in Asia.

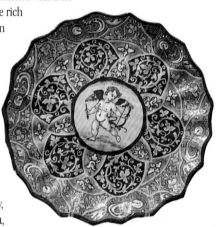

(reproductions of Renaissance designs), bunches of glossy fruit and superb *cesti frutta* (ceramic baskets of fruit to use as table decorations) are among the current range of this Montefiesole ceramicist whose prices are as high as his jars. Plate L55,000, *cesto frutta* from L1,500,000.

Cose del Passato
Via dei Fossi, 3-5r (A2)
☎ **055 29 46 89**
**Every day 10am-1pm,
4-7.30pm, closed Mon. am
and Jul.-Aug.**

This is like an Aladdin's Cave lit by Venetian lanterns, in which Silvana Cappelli has assembled

Manetti & Masini
Piazza N. Sauro, 13r (A2)
☎ **055 28 33 55**
Via Bronzino, 125
☎ **055 70 04 45**
**Every day 10am-12.30pm,
4-7pm, closed Mon. am in
winter and Sat. pm in
summer.**

This antique majolica restorer knows better than anyone the right mixtures of clay and the secrets of the transparency of the glazes. That's why 50 years ago he began reproducing old

pieces from the workshops of Montelupo, Faenza, Pesaro and Della Robbia. Today, his catalogue numbers 300 pieces, but quality has its price – from half a million lire for a dish.

Galleria Machiavelli
**Via Por Santa Maria, 39r
(B2)**
☎ **055 23 98 586**
Mon.-Sat. 9am-7pm.

Huge garden jars, fruit bowls and plates with delightful fruit and flower decoration all the glass and majolica treasures she's uncovered in the four corners of Italy and Europe in the last 25 years. Rare and beautiful 16th-18th-century majolicas are displayed among old pieces of furniture brought back from her travels. If you'd like to talk to her about them, it's better to come in the afternoon.

Ceramiche Italiane
Piazza del Carmine, 14r (A3)
☎ 055 29 21 86
Every day 9.30am-12.30pm, 3.30-7.30pm, 9.30am-7.30pm in summer.

Here you'll find glazed terracotta ceramics you can take out into the garden as soon as the weather turns fine. It comes from Apulia, Tuscany and Sicily, and can be blue and white to match blue Empoli glasses, or decorated with flowers or spots. Also for sale are inexpensive, original masks of Bacchus and red terracotta crescent moons.

Sbigoli Terrecotte
Via San Egidio, 4r (D2)
☎ 055 24 79 713
Every day 9.30am-1pm, 3.30-7.30pm, closed Mon. am or Sat. pm in summer.

Besides the tableware, pots and flower-pot holders

that he throws himself and decorates by hand, he sells marvellous garden pots by Impruneta, the famous factory at the gates of Florence. The nature of the clay soil, which is rich in iron oxide, and the firing at high temperatures makes these pots frost resistant.

Ceramiche Calzaiuoli
Via Calzaiuoli, 8 (C2)
☎ 055 23 82 763
Every day 9am-1pm, 3.30-7.30pm, closed Mon. am or Sat. pm in summer.

Here you can find quite good copies of the objects produced by the major majolica manufacturers of the Renaissance, whether Deruta-type portraits, blue and white vases, the decorative fruit of Montelupo or the cherubs and Virgins of Della Robbia. The forms, on the other hand, have evolved – the lamp bases (L187,000), were unknown in the 16th century but they'll look amazing in your drawing room.

Andreini
Borgo degli Albizi, 63r (C2)
☎ 055 23 40 823
Every day 10.30am-1pm, 4-7.30pm.

Andreini is a supplier to the Italian nobility. These Madonnas, Baroque statues, Classical busts and multi-coloured or natural terracotta fountains and bas reliefs will add an Italian touch to your garden, whatever its size, and will certainly be a talking point at barbecues.

R. B.
Via Romana, 22-24r (A3)
☎ 055 22 80 624
Mon.-Fri. 3.30-7.30pm, Sat. 10am-1pm, 3.30-7.30pm.

This shop, which has the air of a country kitchen, is the result of the collaboration of a ceramicist and an architect who wanted to bring glazed terracotta back into our everyday lives. From the earthenware tiles and the jugs, to garlands of fruit and farm animals, the colours are sunny and the prices very affordable.

STATIONERS AND *LEGATORIE*, EVERYTHING THE TRAVELLING WRITER NEEDS

If you like leather-bound notebooks and photo albums, handmade paper and calligraphy pens, you'll love what you'll find in the many shops and workshops here, where the craft of bookbinding has been passed on from generation to generation. There are plenty of smart souvenirs and lots of gift ideas, including views of Florence in the 19th century.

R. Vannucchi
Via Condotta, 26/28r (C2)
☎ 055 21 67 52
Every day 9.30am-1pm, 3.30-7.30pm.

An old-fashioned stationer's offering a very wide selection of bound albums and notebooks with matching desk accessories. Besides the very fine marbled paper (with patterns repeated on the edges), the series of bees and dragonflies on cards is very appealing. All made using traditional methods by the House of Giannini, which has been renowned for its skill since 1856.

Il Papiro
Lungarno Acciaiuoli, 42r (B2)
Piazza del Duomo, 24r (C2)
☎ 055 21 52 62
Mon.-Sat. 10am-1pm, 2-7pm, Sun. 11am-7pm.

Besides inexpensive, original gifts, such as an eraser with a picture of the Duomo, a trio of miniature books and attractive notebooks covered in marbled paper, you can have business cards printed that will impress your clients. You pay a basic price for the cards, then add L.75,000 for printing costs and L25,000 for despatch to your home address.

Carta &...
Lungarno Acciaiuoli, 40r (B2)
☎ 055 28 31 79
Every day 10am-7.30pm, closed Mon. am in winter, Sat. pm in summer.

Forget e-mail, when you see all the lovely accessories and the

Quick Guide to Marbled Paper

The technique of marbled papermaking, which originated in Japan and Persia, requires a great deal of skill and precision. Colours in suspension in a gelatinous solution are arranged with a comb to form a pattern, which is absorbed by a single sheet of paper. The process must be repeated for each sheet and an effort made to reproduce the same patterns. Most of the 'marbled paper' sold inexpensively at markets is simply printed, but its colours can be quite attractive.

selection of handmade paper, you'll immediately want to write old-fashioned missives with a wax seal or keep a diary in one of the little calfskin-bound books. Prices range from L491,000 for a wooden writing desk to L35,000 for a glass pen.

Lo Scrittoio

Via Guelfa, 112r (C1)
☎ **055 49 65 36**
**Every day 9am-1pm,
3-7.30pm, closed Aug.**

In this little workshop you can see the craftsmen at work, sewing and binding books, notebooks and photo albums. You'll have a choice between calfskin covers (with a very smooth grain) or wild boar (a tougher leather)

and an assortment of of boxes covered in beautiful marbled papers.

Scriptorium

Via dei Servi, 5r (C1)
☎ **055 21 18 04**
Every day 10am-2pm, 3.30-7.30pm, closed Mon. am in winter, Sat. pm in summer.

A little shop full of ideas for personalising your writing paper and books and even the ink, whose colour is linked to a perfume (red-strawberry, turquoise-lotus, etc.). Wonderful calligraphy sets, lovely old-fashioned writing paper, seals with your initials and a cold press for embossing paper – in other words, stacks of nicely-packaged gift ideas.

Il Torchio

Via de' Bardi, 17 (C3)
☎ **055 23 42 862**
Every day 9.30am-1pm, 3.30-7.30pm, closed Mon. am in winter, Sat. pm in summer.

Here you'll find marbled paper of every hue – green, brown, red and blue – covering books, diaries, frames, pencils and even tissue boxes. In a

very feminine atmosphere, you'll find hand-decorated greetings cards, recipe books and heaps of other gifts that can be personalised to order.

Taddei

Via Santa Margherita, 11 (C2)
☎ **055 23 98 960**
Every day 8am-1pm, 3.30-7.30pm, closed Aug.

At Taddei's, you'll find boxes, cases, caskets and desk accessories, entirely handmade from finely-patinated leather, so you'd think they were antiques. The prices are reasonable (L120,000 for a large casket), if you consider the vast amount of work involved.

Ducci

Lungarno Corsini, 24r
☎ **055 21 45 50**
Every day 9am-1pm, 3.30-7.30pm

Fancy a Botticelli, Rosso Fiorentino or Giotto Madonna in your drawing room? The reproductions printed by Ducci are almost as beautiful as the originals, and are distinctly more affordable (L100,000-5 million lire according to the frame). Less famous but nonetheless very beautiful are the etchings of Florence by local artists (L50,000-400,000).

INTERIOR DECORATION AND TABLEWARE

One day, you may get the urge to lay a table Medici-style, with an embroidered tablecloth, engraved crystal glasses, fine Doccia porcelain and embossed silverware. On the other hand, you may want to create a designer setting lit by gorgeous Murano glass lamps. Either way, you'll get plenty of decorative ideas as you search for rare, amusing or beautiful objects at affordable prices in the shops mentioned here.

LIGHTING

Illum

Via XXVII Aprile, 16 (C1)
☎ 055 48 63 28
Every day 9am-1pm, 3.30-7.30pm, closed Mon. am.

The ultimate in designer lighting, offering both leading makes (Fontana Arte and Arteluce) and expert advice, since Illum is responsible for the lighting of churches, historical monuments and the homes of film stars and crowned heads. From the small Murano glass wall lamp at L500,000 to the standard lamp at 2 million, the choice is vast. They'll ship your purchase home.

Mariotti

Via San Spirito, 9 (A3)
☎ 055 28 33 00
Every day 8.30am-12.30pm, 3-7.30pm, closed Aug.

Antique dealers know this shop well. They work the old-fashioned way here, producing magnificent lacquered and gilded Louis XIV and Louis XV chandeliers with hand-cut crystal pendants. Prices vary considerably according to whether the branches are made of crystal or bronze (gilded or otherwise), but there are some very lovely pieces for as little as 1.5 million lire.

Flos

Borgo San Jacopo, 62r (B3)
☎ 055 28 45 09
Mon.-Sat. 9am-1pm, 3.30-7.30pm, closed Mon. am or Sat. pm in summer.

A black marble corridor opening onto the Arno makes the ideal setting for a play on transparency. The Murano glass is bent into the shape of a flared ceiling light, pleated lampshade and arched bedside lamp. Very pure lines by names such as Flos, Arteluce and Flight go perfectly with the vases and bottles by Venini.

DESIGN

Studio Most

Borgo Ognissanti, 46r (A2)
☎ 055 21 32 59
Every day 10am-1.30pm, 3.30-7.30pm, closed Mon. am or Sat. pm in summer.

Yes, it's quite safe to sit on the splendid mooing cow or rather uncomfortable-looking seat.

This highly original furniture designed by the architect Marzio Cecchi has taken the fancy of quite a few people from New York to Saint-Tropez. His unique designs inspired by nature are based on the effects of contrasting materials, fabrics in particular. The modular divan undulates like a snake, the YingYang sofa is ideal for furnishing a corner and the chairs have woven steel backs. The studio will also re-design your home.

Le Stanze

Borgo Ognissanti, 50-52r (A2)
☎ 055 28 89 21
Every day 10am-7.30pm, Mon. 3.30-7.30pm.

Besides the work of the foremost Italian designers (Cappellini, Mondo Campeggi and Porro),

you'll also find heaps of original objects for the home here, such as Indian-style wooden table mats (L65,000), a frying pan in the form of a fried egg (L61,000), a rubber umbrella stand, fine Apulian tableware and an exclusive range of beautiful parchment lamps by the Florentine designer Niccola Falcone.

Controluce

Via della Vigna Nuova, 89r (B2)
☎ 055 23 98 871
Every day 9am-7.30pm, closed Mon. am or Sat. pm in summer.

Why not fix a vase to your window with a suction pad, wear a watch on your finger, write with a sardine or light a cigarette with a helicopter? If these ideas grab you, you'll find plenty more madly

original objects in this tiny shop. In terms of design, don't miss the great lamps by Rizzatto and the Storm watches.

WORLD OBJECTS

Oltrefrontiera

Via Mazzetta, 14r (A3)
☎ 055 21 34 96
Tue.-Sat. 10am-8pm, closed 15-31 Aug.

Large Mexican jars, Indian wrought-iron objects, English colonial armchairs, Filipino lampshades made of recycled paper, Vietnamese lacquered bamboo dishes and Indonesian coconut dishes – furniture and objects old and new from around the world that will add a touch of the exotic to your home at very little cost.

Cose dal Mondo

Via San Niccoló, 121 (C3)
☎ 055 23 42 685
Every day 9.30am-1pm, 3.30-7.30pm.

On the ground floor of the Palazzo Mozzi you'll find a collection of crockery and utensils brought back by a curious traveller from all over the world. A Czech grill with a vertical revolving spit sits alongside an Iranian pressure cooker and a gorgeous Portuguese dinner service stands side-by-side with Vietnamese bowls. The *tira-spaghetti* spoon and the chest with a pasta storage drawer are obviously Italian. Buying something here won't mean breaking the bank.

tablecloth and napkins, a lace-trimmed bathrobe and towels for her and a silk paisley-patterned dressing-gown for him. Prices vary according to whether the items are hand or machine-embroidered and the lace is hand or machine-made. There's a line of lisle underwear for those who feel the cold.

Un Jardin... en Plus

Via del Parione,32r (B2)
☎ 055 28 70 47
9.30am-1pm, 3.30-7.30pm, closed Mon. am or Sat. pm in summer.

For the bedroom, variations on the theme of bees, fruit and flowers on sheer curtains, sheets and towels by Maestro Raphael. For the drawing room, large glass bowls, gilded wooden frames, wrought-iron chandeliers and pretty Italian earthenware.

HOUSEHOLD LINEN

Mazzoni

Via Orsanmichele, 14r (C2)
☎ 055 21 51 53
Every day 9am-1pm, 3.30-7.30pm, closed Mon. am or Sat.pm in summer.

In the shadow of Orsanmichele, the former wool-working district, this old shop, lined with wooden shelves and drawers, carries on the tradition of Florentine expertise in the area of fabrics and embroidery. You can get embroidered and monogrammed linen or silk sheets, quilted blue

and gold bedspreads, delicate table and bathroom linen, floral aprons with matching tea-cloths, damask by the metre/yard and lots of sound advice.

G. P.

Piazza Duomo, 62r (C2)
☎ 055 28 46 28
Every day 9am-1pm, 3.30-7.30pm, closed Mon. am.

Complete your wedding trousseau here with a lace-edged tablecloth, Flanders cloth with a sprinkling of woven flowers, a hand-hemmed

GLASS, PORCELAIN AND SILVER

Archimede Seguso

Via Tornabuoni, 65r (B2)
☎ 055 28 34 67
Every day 10am-7.30pm, closed Mon. am.

If you missed it in Venice, you'll find a very complete selection of pieces by Archimede Seguso here. Seguso is the oldest and most famous Murano master glass-maker, whose work is exhibited in museums all over the world. Expect to pay from L.98,000 for a small vase to 3 million lire for a six-branched chandelier.

GET CONNECTED!

If you've bought a lamp, make sure it has a suitable plug. If it's a standard Italian flat three-pin plug, you may need to buy an adaptor that will also come in handy for plugging in the designer household appliances you've filled your cases with.

Paola Locchi

**Via D. Burchiello, 10
(12 bus,
off map)
☎ 055 22
98 371
Mon.-Fri.
8.30am-1pm,
3-6.30pm,
closed Aug.**

This place isn't only for those clumsy people who've broken the stopper of a Liberty carafe or a Baccarat crystal dish. In this workshop established in the 19th century, highly-specialised craftsmen grind, cut, polish and engrave glass in the old-fashioned way. Performing miracles, they succeed in reproducing crystal objects of every kind. Here you can find a pair of Bohemian candlesticks at L120,000, a Medici glass at L220,000 and many other modestly-priced marvels.

Cassetti

**Via Strozzi,7-9r (B2)
☎ 055 29 45 77
Every day 10am-1pm,
3.30-7.30pm, closed Mon.
am or Sat. pm in summer.**

Behind these sumptuous silver objects lies the experience of three generations of silversmiths who have in their turn called on the best Italian designers to create new styles of cutlery, tea and coffee services, candlesticks and peppermills. These elegant pieces will light up your table, whether you prefer antiques or designer objects.

Richard-Ginori

**Via Rondinelli, 17r (B2)
☎ 055 21 00 41
Every day 10am-7pm,
closed Mon. am or Sat. pm
in summer.**

The Doccia factory, one of the oldest in Europe, has been producing the Richard Ginori make of fine porcelain since 1896. As well as reproductions of old designs, you'll find the new collections designed by Trussardi and the very lovely Art Deco line by Gio Ponti. They also make very chic personalised dinner services to order, decorated with a view of your property, your coat of arms or a monogram.

Brandimarte

**Via L. Bartolini, 8 (A2)
☎ 055 23 93 81
Mon.-Fri. 9.30am-1pm,
3.30-7.30pm, Sat. 9am-1pm.**

Pieces made the traditional way by a small silver workshop that started with the production of everyday silverware – pitchers, mugs, milk jugs and baskets. Since then, the range has been extended to include all kinds of solid silver objects with decoration largely inspired by nature – vines, ears of corn, flowers and birds, stamped and engraved in wreaths and garlands.

BARGAIN CORNER

While the sale of secondhand clothes may not really have taken off yet in Florence, you'll find quite a few shops selling ends of ranges and designer accessories for 50% less than in Via de' Tornabuoni. Don't be surprised if you see quite wealthy Florentines shopping here – they don't want

to miss a bargain. If it's shoes you're after, you'll have to wait for the sales if you don't like clumpy footwear.

One Price

Borgo Ognissanti, 74r (A2)
☎ **055 28 46 74**
Every day 9am-1pm, 3.30-7.30pm, closed Mon. am or Sat. pm in summer.

A unisex warehouse selling Italian seventies gear for 20% less all year round. If you look hard, you may even come across a little linen jacket or great bomber jacket at a really unbeatable price.

Il Guarda-Roba

Via Giuseppe Verdi, 28r (corner of Via Ghibellina, D2)
☎ **055 247 82 50**
Every day 9.30am-1pm, 3.30-7.30pm, closed Mon. am.

Whether their style is sporty or smart, men and women alike will find something to please them at this shop which sells secondhand clothes and bankrupt stock, all in good condition. Fendi, Armani, Versace and Moschino, all the big names

at knockdown prices, as well as lots of well-cut clothes and leather jackets. A Versace ladies' suit sells for L560,000, a leather skirt for L185,000.

Stroll

Via Romana, 78r (A3)
☎ **055 22 91 44**
Every day 9.30am-1.30pm, 3.30-7.30pm, closed Mon. am.

STROLL

Whatever your age or size, Giovanna Mantelli will find you an outfit you like at a price that's right. Mixing with flair big-brand ends of ranges and ethnic clothes, in particular Japanese and Indian, this designer, with a finger firmly on the fashion pulse, will supply you with all the ingredients you need for a sporty, laid-back or glamorous look.

Ultra

Via XXVII Aprile, 37r (C1)
☎ 055 48 98 61
Every day 10am-1pm, 3.30-7.30pm, closed Mon. am.

For 15 to 20-year-olds, a complete Italian street and sportswear look (DHline, Worldribe and X-Age), with tough workmen's boots to match. You can buy a complete outfit, from check cap to ultra-wide cotton dungarees, for L120,000. Fantastic!

Docksteps Store

Via dei Pecori, 35r (B2)
☎ 055 28 21 93
Tue.-Sat. 10am-1pm, 3.30-7.30pm, Mon. 2.30-7.30pm.

Last season's ends of ranges and seconds at knockdown prices for bikers and anyone who like biker boots with big, shiny buckles. For the girls on the pillion behind them, there are sporty styles with a bit more class.

Grandi Firme

Via dei Lamberti, 16r (C2)
☎ 055 21 35 99
Via del Trebbio, 10r
☎ 23 81 527
Every day 9.30am-1.30pm, 3.30-7.30pm, closed Mon. am or Sat. pm Jul.-Aug.

Unless you're a fashion junkie, you won't mind wearing clothes by Dolce & Gabbana, Moschino, Marina Rinaldi, Valentino or Max Mara that are a year or two out of date. With the money you save (40-50%), you'll be able to buy twice as much. The only problem is the sizes, which are mainly (Italian) women's 42-44 and men's 50. If these don't fit, you can always fall back on the hats and jumpers.

High-Class

Via Por Santa Maria (B3)
☎ 055 21 03 19
Every day 9am-7pm.

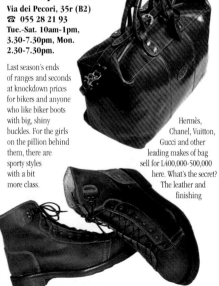

Hermès, Chanel, Vuitton, Gucci and other leading makes of bag sell for L400,000-500,000 here. What's the secret? The leather and finishing are of very high quality but the bags are (good) imitations made by highly-skilled workers. It's best to think twice before buying one, though – the possession of such fakes can earn you a fine, if you are unlucky.

Coin

Via del Corso, 59r (C2)
☎ 055 28 05 31
Mon.-Sat. 9.30am-8pm, Sun. 11am-8pm.

There are plenty of bargains to be had in this department store – for women, a collection of silk clothes and pretty underwear (including well-known brands) at ultra-low prices – for men, underwear and pyjamas. There are great kid's clothes, too (trousers L40,000). The bargain corner has last season's clothes all year round.

La Belle Epoque

Borgo degli Albizi, 48r
Tue.-Sat. 10am-1pm, 3.30-7.30pm, Mon. 2.30-7.30pm

In one of the few secondhand clothes shops in Florence, men and women alike are sure to find what they're looking for among a wide choice of secondhand clothes and accessories, all in very good condition. Take a look a little further on in no. 78 as well, where the clothes are trendier.

Nightlife Practicalities

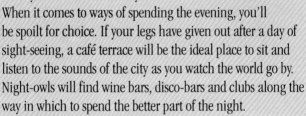

Florence is as beautiful by night as by day. A stroll along the banks of the Arno will show you the best of the city. When it comes to ways of spending the evening, you'll be spoilt for choice. If your legs have given out after a day of sight-seeing, a café terrace will be the ideal place to sit and listen to the sounds of the city as you watch the world go by. Night-owls will find wine bars, disco-bars and clubs along the way in which to spend the better part of the night.

WHERE TO GO

Thanks to the Teatro Verdi and the former Muratte prison, Santa Croce is a dynamic district, with plenty of wine bars and friendly cafés. In summer, many live performances are staged in the historic city centre, especially in the Piazza della Signoria and sometimes in the Piazza Santissima Annunziata. On the other side of the Arno, the San Spirito and San Frediano districts are very lively all year round, both outdoors, in the squares where you can also have a meal in the summer, and indoors, in the trendy bars. The clubs, however, are spread all over Florence, the most popular being in the city centre and Cascine park.

WHAT TO WEAR IN THE EVENING

If you intend to go to an opera at the newly refurbished Teatro Goldoni or the Teatro Comunale, or eat in a fashionable restaurant, don't forget to pack something dressy to wear and a tie. There aren't really any rules about what to wear elsewhere, and the Florentine look fluctuates between the *molto chic* of the over-thirties to the trendy casual wear of the young.

NIGHTCLUBBING

Most of the clubs and some disco-bars insist you have a membership card *(tessera)* valid for a year. Apart from a few more exclusive places, where you have to be sponsored by a member, you can buy a card (costing L20,000 at least, including a free drink) at the door. If you don't want to end up at a bar packed with tourists, go to some of the trendy bars (Cabiria and Dolce Vita) to find out the latest in-places.

For dancing, the Florentines prefer disco-bars to nightclubs. Here you can have a drink, talk, meet people and dance to good music – either live or mixed by DJs. At the risk of disappointing techno and house fans, it has to be said that Italian tastes tend towards Latino rhythms, reggae and funk. If discos appeal to you, go around midnight if you're looking for a good atmosphere.

CULTURAL CALENDAR

If you want to find out the dates of major events before you leave, write or fax the **Azienda di Promozione Turistica di Firenze** (Via Manzoni, 16-50 121 Firenze, ☎ 055 23 320 ⊜ 055 23 46 286), who will send you information about Florence and Tuscany. Alternatively, you can consult the Internet (www.informacitta.net.).

SAFETY

If you stay in the lively city centre, you won't be in much danger except from pickpockets, who are very skilful. It's best to take the precaution of leaving valuables in the hotel safe, and when you're doing the rounds of the sites, bars and discos, only carry what you need. Take care on buses and around Santa Maria Novella Station. Stay alert in the neighbourhood of Cascine park, where there are a number of fashionable places.

La Repubblica publishes a supplement containing a complete list of cultural events every Thursday. You'll also find a few pages of information in Florence's daily newspaper, *La Nazione*. Complete information about cultural events is given in the monthly publication *Firenze Spettacolo*, which has a supplement in English, *Florenscope*. It also contains a selection of vouchers entitling you to free tickets or reductions for various performances. Free, and available from hotels, the brochure *Florence Concierge Information*, which is updated monthly, gives a glimpse of day and nightlife in Florence. The magazine *Events,* which is designed for foreigners living in Florence, is a good source of information and has the advantage of being written in English (on sale at kiosks or available from

HOW TO BOOK SEATS FOR A PERFORMANCE

To book concert or theatre seats once you get to Florence or from abroad, contact the **Box Office** (Via Faenza, 139r, ☎ 055 21 08 04, or Chiasso de' Soldanieri, 8r, ☎ 055 21 94 02). If you're connected to the Internet, look for the **Weekend a Firenze** web site (www.weekendafirenze.com) which sells tickets for concerts, ballets, etc. If you decide to go to the theatre at the last moment, consult your hotel porter, who will have a list of seats available for the various concerts and performances and can book them for you.

large hotels). Finally, you can consult the monthly calendar at the Tourist Information Office in the Via Cavour.

CONCERTS, THEATRE, OPERA AND DANCE

From September to April, the ballets, symphonic and operatic concerts and plays are mainly set in the Teatro Verdi and Teatro Comunale, but performances also take place in beautiful Florentine churches and *cenacoli* (former convent refectories).

In spring, the *Maggio Musicale* (20 April to 20 June) opens the festival season. This anthology of high-quality performances is of interest to music and avant-garde theatre lovers alike, as well as to jazz fans. In June, the *Rossini Filarmonica di Firenze* stages concerts in the Piazza della Signoria. There are also a multitude of open-air events (cinema, ballets, recitals and concerts)in summer in the city's most beautiful palaces, squares and gardens, on the river Arno and in the Roman theatre at Fiesole in the hills of Florence.

Teatro Verdi
**Via Ghibellina, 99
(Santa Croce)
☎ 055 21 23 20
Performance at 8pm
Tickets L10,000-25,000.**

As the seat of the Regional Orchestra of Tuscany, the Teatro Verdi stages concerts of symphonic music, recitals, chamber music and ancient and contemporary music through-

out the year. It also hosts concerts of rock and modern music.

Teatro Comunale
**Corso Italia, 16
(Porta al Prato)
☎ 055 21 11 58/
055 21 35 35
Performances at 12.30pm,
3pm and 8pm, tickets
L30,000-100,000.**

This venue consists of various auditoria in which classical music concerts, ballets and operatic performances are staged from September to April. The main events of the Maggio Musicale take place here.

Teatro Goldoni
**Via dei Serragli, 109
(Porta Romana)
☎ 055 27 791
Performance at 8.30pm,
Sat. 3.30pm, tickets
L40,000-100,000.**

Restored at last after ten years' work, this 18th-century jewel has returned to its former glory to house performances of opera and *bel canto*.

Orsanmichele
**Via Calzaiuoli (Centre)
(bookings Via E. Poggi, 6)
☎ 055 78 33 74
Performance at 9pm
Tickets L20,000.**

From April to October, this church alternates with the Badia

Fiorentina (Via del Proconsolo), to house concerts of classical music given by the Orchestra da Camera Fiorentina.

Teatro della Pergola
**Via della Pergola, 18
(Centre)
☎ 055 24 79 651/2
Performance at 8.45pm,
Sat.-Sun. 3.45pm,
Tickets L20,000-35,000.**

Pirandello, Molière, Shakespeare, Ionesco, Commedia dell'Arte, tragedy and mime – in other words, good performances of classical theatre in Italian, as well as screenings of old films and concerts of symphonic music, all held in a sumptuous 18th-century setting.

Teatro Puccini
**Piazza Puccini
(Cascine – bus 17)
☎ 055 36 20 67
Performance at 9pm,
Sun. 5pm
Tickets L23,000-28,000.**

Modern productions by a variety of theatre companies ranging from comedy to satire, and from plays by well-known authors to magic shows.

Teatro di Rifredi

**Via Victor Emanuele, 303
(Rifredi – bus 25)
☎ 055 42 20 361
Performance at 9pm,
Sun. 4.30pm
Tickets L20,000.**

Companies from all over Italy perform plays by Italian and foreign playwrights.

VARIETY CAFÉS AND JAZZ CLUBS

Jazz Club

**Via Nuova de' Caccini, 3
(corner of Borgo Pinti)
☎ 055 24 97 00
Concert at 9.30pm
Membership card L10,000.**

For twenty years, the Jazz Club situated near the Pergola theatre has been one of the pillars of Florentine life, frequented by students and older jazz fans alike. There are concerts and singers every evening, with jam sessions on Tuesdays.

Teatro Tenda

**Lungarno A. Moro, 3
(Madonnone – bus 14)
☎ 055 65 04 112
Concert at 9pm
Tickets L25,000.**

If you like Eros Ramazzotti and Paolo Conte, the concerts here will enable you to discover other Italian composers and lyricists.

Sala Vanni

**Piazza del Carmine, 19
(San Frediano)
☎ 055 28 73 47
Concert at 9pm
Tickets L20,000.**

A fairly eclectic programme ranging from classical music to contemporary rock by way of jazz and traditional songs.

Teatro Verdi

**Via Ghibellina, 99
(Santa Croce)
☎ 055 21 23 20
Tickets L10,000-25,000.**

Concerts by Italian and foreign crooners.

Tenax

**Via Pratese, 46
(Peretola – bus 29)
☎ 055 30 81 60
Concert at 9/10pm
Tickets, L15,000-25,000.**

Tenax is renowned throughout Italy for the quality of its concerts and the guest artists who perform here three or four times a week. At the weekend, it's a disco frequented mainly by students, who come to the Saturday College Party in particular. At the heart of the Tenax is the Tube, a club with a science fantasy decor, that plays jungle, drum'n'bass and avant-garde music.

Auditorium Flog

**Via M. Mercati, 24
(Rifredi – bus 25)
☎ 055 48 71 45
Concert at 10.30pm
Tickets L5,000-25,000.**

This showcase of world culture houses the international festival of Folk Music (*Musica dei Popoli*) and cinematographic events (*Film Etno-musicale*). Thursdays and Fridays see a wide variety of concerts ranging from neo-punk to rock, with live music, hip-hop and rock at the weekend.

Pongo

**Via Verdi, 57r (Santa Croce)
☎ 055 23 47 880
Every day except Sun.
4.30pm-2am, closed
in summer. Concert at
10.30pm, entry free.**

Rockers come here for concerts during the week and to dance at the weekend. In the afternoon you can tune in to TV programmes from all over the world or surf the Internet. Happy hour is at 7pm.

WINE BARS

Le Volpi e l'Uva

**Piazza dei Rossi, 1r
☎ 055 23 98 132
Every day except Sun.
10am-8pm.**

A discreet place a stone's throw from the Ponte Vecchio. A wine expert and a wine waiter have pooled their knowlege to select forty or so wines to taste with cheese or charcuterie. A warm welcome and a very reasonable bill.

Enoteca de' Giraldi

**Via de' Giraldi
☎ 055 21 65 18
Every day exc. Sun.
11am-4pm, 6pm-1am.**

A *vinaino* offering less well known but no less interesting D.O.C.G. (*denominazione di origine controllata*) wines

from small vineyards all over Tuscany. Tasting is by the glass with plates of charcuterie, local cheese or delicious *crostini*. A selection of dessert wines and grappas also figure on the menu.

Enoteca Le Barrique

Via del Leone, 40r
☎ 055 22 41 92
Every day exc. Mon. 4.30pm-1am, Fri.-Sat. until 2am.

This was one of the first traditional bars in the very pleasant district of San Frediano to be turned into a wine bar offering a menu to satisfy every hunger. Among its specialities are a cheese board, white truffle or mushroom pâté, fish and meat dishes, as well as a cellar boasting 400 wines.

BARS

Eskimo

Via dei Canacci, 12r
(Santa Maria Novella)
Every day exc. Mon.
9.30pm-3.30am.

A small club hosted by Francesco Cofone, a Calabrian singer who

makes musical instruments and a stage available to talented young musicians who are feeling inspired. Southern cuisine is served with sangria and cocktails to live background music every evening.

Porfirio Rubirosa

Viale Strozzi, 18/20r
(Santa Maria Novella)
☎ 055 49 09 65
Every day exc. Mon. 7am-2am.

Arranged on two floors and a clever mixture of bistrot and high tech, this very smart place opposite the Fortezza da Basso is a leading Florentine nightspot hosted by Andrea and Marco Angelini. Very trendy clientele. Snacks according to availability (charcuterie, cheese, etc.).

at aperitif time, when everyone crowds onto the terrace. Music mixed by a DJ on Thursday and Friday nights, and light refreshments.

Dolce Vita

Piazza del Carmine
(Santo Frediano)
☎ 055 28 45 95
In winter 5pm-1.30am,
Sat. 5pm-2.30am,
in summer 11-1.30am.

This chrome and black marble-clad bar, the most glamorous in Florence, has become the symbol of the *movida fiorentina*. An effective cocktail of disco-bar, small exhibitions, mini-concerts, aperitifs and gossip, it's particularly lively at the weekend and

Girasol

Via del Romito, 1r
(Fortezza da Basso)
☎ 055 47 49 48
Every day exc. Mon.
7am-2.30pm, closed Aug.

A corner of Latin America in a cellar, a kind of tropical beach where you dance to Afro-Cuban and Brazilian rhythms, Latino-jazz, soul, reggae and samba. A very warm atmosphere helped along by Adalmir Pinheiro's cocktails – *batida al guaranà*, *caipirinha* and the rest.

Cabiria

**Piazza Santo Spirito
(Santo Spirito)
☎ 055 21 57 32
Every day exc. Tue. 9.30-1am.
Fri.-Sat. 9.30-2am.**

Café CABIRIA

With a background of soul, jazz, and funk mixed by a DJ in the evenings (Thursdays to Sundays), this is one of the young Florentines' favourite places, featuring tables outside in the Piazza Santo Spirito in summer, a warm interior, delicious *zakuskis* and fast food at any time of day. And, despite its reputation as a very trendy bar, the prices are totally democratic.

La Posterula

**Piazza Davanzati, 3r
(Centre)
☎ 055 23 81 958
Every day 7.30pm-2am,
Fri.-Sat. 7.30pm-3am.**

Have a bite to eat at lunchtime, and in the evening, enjoy a disco-bar hosted by a DJ with eclectic tastes. Pre-disco atmosphere on Tuesdays, trip-hop, jungle and trance music on Wednesdays, rap, reggae and ragga on Thursdays, Groove Party on Fridays, Bacco's Party on Saturdays, and theme evenings on Sundays.

Sotto Sopra

**Via dei Serragli, 48r
(Santo Spirito)
☎ 055 28 23 40
Every day exc. Sun.
6pm-1.30am.**

Upstairs is a small American bar, where you can sip potent cocktails; downstairs is a dance floor, where you can flirt or dance the night away to music mixed by a different DJ every evening. Clientele range from 18-30, and entry is free.

Nirvana

**Via Sacchetti, 9r
(Piazza delle Cure)
☎ 055 50 01 615
Every day 7pm-1.30am.**

Subdued lighting, mandalas on the walls, waterfalls, incense burners and Indian music welcome you to the first New Age nightclub in Florence. Those who aren't blown away by the atmosphere nibble vegetarian talis made from tofu accompanied by a choice of dozens of varieties of tea or, more prosaically, beer and cocktails.

Rex

**Via Fiesolana, 25r
(Sant' Ambrogio)
☎ 055 24 80 331
Every day exc. Tue.
5pm-1.30am.**

The baroque, Gaudí-style decor, a blend of terracotta and metal, makes this one of the most attractive bars in the city, where you can always find someone to talk to at aperitif time or late at night, when it's in full swing. Good music, sometimes live.

Conversion tables for clothes shopping

Women's sizes

Shirts/dresses

U.K	U.S.A	EUROPE
8	6	36
10	8	38
12	10	40
14	12	42
16	14	44
18	16	46

Sweaters

U.K	U.S.A	EUROPE
8	6	44
10	8	46
12	10	48
14	12	50
16	14	52

Shoes

U.K	U.S.A	EUROPE
3	5	36
4	6	37
5	7	38
6	8	39
7	9	40
8	10	41

Men's sizes

Shirts

U.K	U.S.A	EUROPE
14	14	36
$14^{1/2}$	$14^{1/2}$	37
15	15	38
$15^{1/2}$	$15^{1/2}$	39
16	16	41
$16^{1/2}$	$16^{1/2}$	42
17	17	43
$17^{1/2}$	$17^{1/2}$	44
18	18	46

Suits

U.K	U.S.A	EUROPE
36	36	46
38	38	48
40	40	50
42	42	52
44	44	54
46	46	56

Shoes

U.K	U.S.A	EUROPE
6	8	39
7	9	40
8	10	41
9	10.5	42
10	11	43
11	12	44
12	13	45

More useful conversions

1 centimetre	0.39 inches	1 inch	2.54 centimetres
1 metre	1.09 yards	1 yard	0.91 metres
1 kilometre	0.62 miles	1 mile	1. 61 kilometres
1 litre	1.76 pints	1 pint	0.57 litres
1 gram	0.35 ounces	1 ounce	28.35 grams
1 kilogram	2.2 pounds	1 pound	0.45 kilograms

This guide was written by **Katherine Vanderhaeghe**,
who would like to thank **Lara Fantoni** from the Florence Tourist Office,
Ludovica Villoresi, Paola Cecchi and **Romano Romoli**.
Translator and copy editor **Margaret Rocques**
Series editor **Liz Coghill**
Additional research and assistance **Vanessa Dowell, Jeremy Smith** and
Christine Bell

Photo acknowledgements

Inside pages
All photographs were taken by **Éric Guillot**, except for the following:

Alex Cholet: p. 10 (c.l.), p. 11 (t.c.). **Photothèque Hachette**: p. 20 (t.r.), p. 21 (c.l.), p. 23, 24 (t.r.), p. 25 (b.r.), p. 30 (b.l.), 31 (c.r.), 109 (c.r.) **Lorenzo Villoresi**: p.37 (c.l.), ©A. Coppitz p. 68 (b.r.) **Casa dei Tessuti**: p. 43 (c.r.) **Salvatore Ferragamo**: p. 50 (b.r.), p. 99 (c.c.) **Luciano Mario Rossi**: p. 59 (c.l.) **Leather School**: p. 61 (t.l.) **Baglioni**: p. 75 (c.c.) **Hotel City**: p. 75 (b.r.) **Grand Hotel**: p. 75 (b.l.) **Il Cibreo** © **Guido Mannucci**: p. 79 (b.l.) **Bianzino**: p. 93 (t.c.) **Marcello Buccellati, DB Studio**: p. 100 (b.l.) **Settepassi, Faraone**: p. 100 (c.c.) **Bartolozzi**: p. 108 (b.r.) **Bruno Gallori Turchi**: p. 109 (b.l.) **Mazzoni**: p. 116 (t.l.)

Front cover
Éric Guillot: t.l., t.r., c.c., c.r., b.l.; **Stock Image C. Bouvier**: t.c.; **Stock Image Jim Boorman**: c.r. (foreground); **Stock Image A. Rohmer**: b.m.; **Hémisphères Stéphane Frances**: c.l.; **Photothèque Hachette**: b.r.

Back cover
Éric Guillot: t.r., c.c., b.l.; **Hémisphères Laurent Giraudou**: c.l.

Illustrations: Monique Prudent

Cartography: © Hachette Tourisme

First published in the United Kingdom in 2000 by Hachette UK

Distributed in the United States of America by Sterling Publishing Co., Inc.
387 Park Avenue South, New York, NY 10016-8810

A CIP catalogue for this book is available from the British Library

ISBN 1 84202 010 2

Hachette UK, Cassell & Co., The Orion Publishing Group, Wellington House, 125 Strand,
London WC2R 0BB

Printed and bound in Italy by Milanostampa S.P.A.

If you're staying on a little longer and would like to try some new places, the following pages will provide you with a wide choice of hotels, restaurants and bars, listed by district. Though you can just turn up at the door of a restaurant and have a meal (except in the most prestigious establishments), don't forget to book your hotel several days in advance (see p. 66). Prices quoted are a guide only. Enjoy your stay!

STAYING ON
A LITTLE LONGER

The following hotels are listed strictly in accordance with the official Italian classification. Prices are given for a double room with en-suite bathroom or shower and breakfast. These are high-season prices, and should be used as a guideline only. If you go during the low season, you can pay significantly less. For further information on hotels in Florence, see Rooms and Restaurants (p. 72).

Santa Maria Novella

Bonciani ***
Via dei Panzani, 17
☎ 055 26 090
📠 055 26 85 12
Around L210,000.
A 15th-century palace a few steps from the Duomo with its own car park and a games room for children.

Le Vigne **
Piazza Santa Maria Novella, 24
☎ 055 29 44 49
📠 055 23 02 263
Around L180,000.
One of these 15th-century palace's bedrooms is prettily decorated with frescoes, as is the breakfast room. You'll enjoy a pleasant rest under its coffered ceilings.

Albergo Polo Nord*
Via dei Panzani, 7
☎ 055 28 79 52
Around L120,000.
A small, modestly-priced pension that's spotless and welcoming in the heart of the historic centre between the Church of Santa Maria Novella and the Duomo.

Piazza Goldoni

Fiorentina *
Via de' Fossi, 12
☎ 055 21 95 30
📠 055 28 71 05
(closed at Christmas)
Around L110,000.
A hotel in a former palace a few steps from the historic centre with large, pleasant rooms overlooking a garden. Run by a charming French couple.

Duomo

Brunelleschi ****
Piazza S. Elisabetta, 3
☎ 055 29 03 11
📠 055 21 96 53
Around L480,000.
This luxury hotel midway between the Duomo and the Piazza della Signoria offers all the advantages of its category in a magnificent historic building.

De la Ville ****
Piazza Antinori, 1
☎ 055 23 81 805
📠 055 23 81 809
Around L450,000.
You won't get tired carrying your shopping back to this hotel just next to the most elegant street in the city. A fine building with a cosmopolitan clientele.

Mona Lisa ****
Borgo Pinti, 27
☎ 055 24 79 751
📠 055 24 79 755
Around L400,000.
Luxury comes at a price, but you won't regret it in this sumptuous period palace with frescoes, superb coffered ceilings and rooms overlooking a walled garden. A unique hotel that will take you to the heart of the Renaissance.

Pierre ****
Via de' Lamberti, 5
☎ 055 21 62 18
📠 055 23 96 573
Around L400,000.
A stone's throw from the Piazza della Repubblica and its well-known cafés, this listed building guarantees you a quiet stay in the midst of the Florentine bustle.

Pendini ***
Via Strozzi, 2
☎ 055 21 11 70
📠 055 28 18 07
Around L280,000.
A quiet, comfortable hotel in a 19th-century building. A little out of the way, but just behind the Piazza della Repubblica.

De' Lanzi ***
Via delle Oche, 11
☎ 055 28 80 43
📠 055 28 80 43
Around L260,000.
A hotel with the advantage of soundproofing and air-conditioning five minutes from the Duomo in the heart of the historic city centre.

Duomo ***
Piazza Duomo, 1
☎ 055 21 99 22
📠 055 21 64 10
Around L220,000.
This hotel has probably the best view of the cathedral in the city, so you can study every detail of its marvellous architecture from close quarters both night and day. It also offers a friendly welcome.

Pensione Maxim *
Via de' Medici, 4
☎ 055 21 74 74
📠 055 28 37 29
Around L140,000.
A dozen clean, quiet rooms and a warm welcome. This peaceful little pension in a pedestrianised street is as central as it can be. However, its one major advantage is a supervised car park nearby.

Ponte Vecchio

Lungarno ****
Borgo San Jacopo, 14
☎ 055 27 26 11
📠 055 26 84 37
Around L400,000.
From your window in this hotel on the Oltrarno, you'll have one of the most beautiful views in the world – the cupola of the Duomo silhouetted against the gentle hills of Fiesole.

Torre Guelfa **
Borgo SS. Apostoli, 8
☎ 055 23 96 338
📠 055 23 98 577
Around L250,000.
The prices rise a little steeply in this hotel in the high season, but it's set in a former palace, just next to the old port and offers a friendly welcome.

Ognissanti

Casa del Lago **
Lungarno Amerigo Vespucci, 58
☎ 055 21 61 41
📠 055 21 41 49
Around L150,000.
With 15 or so rooms and an outstanding view of the Arno, modest prices and excellent service, this is a place to tell your friends about.

Pitti

Pensione La Scaletta **
Via Guicciardini, 13n
☎ 055 28 30 28/
055 21 42 55
☏ 055 28 95 62
Around L180,000.
This hotel is much sought after. It's in a charming 15th-century palace, with a view of the Boboli gardens from the terrace. If you decide to stay here, remember to book well in advance.

Stazione

Boston ***
Via Guelfa, 68
☎ 055 49 67 47
☏ 055 47 09 34
Around L230,000.
This modern hotel with a small garden near the Piazza dell' Indipendenza is a practical choice.

Monica Hotel **
Via Faenza, 66
☎ 055 28 17 06
☏ 055 28 38 04
Around 170,000.
A charming little local hotel that's recently been renovated and equipped with all mod cons. It has a small terrace that makes for a very pleasant stay.

Petrarca **
Via Fiume, 20
☎ 055 23 81 209
☏ 055 21 64 45
Around L160,000.
A simple, unpretentious hotel with all the necessary facilities 50m/yds from the station and 5 minutes from the Duomo.

Pensione Accademia*
Via Faenza, 7
☎ 055 29 34 51
Around L160,000.
The main advantage of this very central pension is its peaceful atmosphere, as well as its old-fashioned decor with painted beams. Telephone and television in all rooms.

San Marco

Il Guelfo Bianco ***
Via Cavour, 57r
☎ 055 28 83 30
☏ 055 29 52 03
Around L320,000.

A vast well-kept hotel with large, quiet rooms. Very practical for those who wish to devote a short stay to the painting of Fra Angelico, as the convent is next door. The hotel also has smaller, less expensive rooms

Cimabue **
Via B. Lupi, 7
☎ 055 47 19 89
☏ 055 47 56 01
Around L170,000
This fine building dating from the turn of the century 800m/yd. north of the Duomo has a few charming rooms whose ceilings are decorated with frescoes.

San Lorenzo

Palazzo Benci ***
Piazza Madonna Aldobrandini, 3
☎ 055 21 38 48
☏ 055 28 83 08
(closed around 15 Aug.)
Around L280,000
This hotel is right next to the big, lively market and Capelle Medicee. It's housed in a 16th-century palace and has a very pretty garden, planted with trees.

Piazza Beccaria

Orcagna **
Via Orcagna, 57/59
☎ 055 66 99 59
Around L160,000
An unpretentious modern hotel with a small garden where you'll be given a warm welcome. Ten minutes from the centre by 14 bus.

Bologna **
Via Orcagna, 50
☎ 055 67 83 59
☏ 055 66 12 41
Around L130,000.
Despite being situated in the city's other shopping centre, this is a quiet hotel with all the mod cons.

Piazza del Prato

Villa Medici *****
Via Il Prato, 42
☎ 055 23 81 331
☏ 055 23 81 336
Around L780,000.
A luxury hotel with a garden, a swimming pool and even a children's games room, just next to the pretty Cascine park.

Montebello Spendid ****
Via Montebello, 60
☎ 055 23 98 501
🅕 055 21 18 67
Around L470,000.
This hotel, arranged round a delightfully calm interior garden, is just a stone's throw from the city theatre and park in a street parallel to the Arno.

Bellosguardo

Torre di Bellosguardo ****
Via Roti Michelozzi, 2
☎ 055 22 98 145
🅕 055 22 90 08
Around L480,000.
This charming hotel on the little green Bellosguardo Hill overlooking the south of Florence has a swimming pool and garden. You'd think you were in the country even though you're very close to the bustle of the city.

Piazza Alberti

Da Verrazzano ***
Via di Bellariva, 18
☎ 055 67 97 66
🅕 055 67 76 92
Around L220,000.
This hotel, very close to the Arno and a few minutes from the historic centre, is in the residential district of Florence. It's been entirely renovated and offers all mod cons, and you can reach the centre in 10 minutes by 14 bus.

San Miniato al Monte

Villa Liberty ***
Viale Michelangiolo, 40
☎ 055 68 10 581
🅕 055 68 12 595
Around L280,000.
A magnificent patrician villa, entirely decorated in the Liberty style and with a beautiful garden. It overlooks the city though it's barely a quarter of an hour from the centre.

HOTELS

Bargello

I Ghibellini
Piazza S. Pier
Maggiore, 10r
☎ 055 21 44 24
Closed Wed.
Around L35 000.
This restaurant is in a lovely medieval building is frequented by Florentines and is always packed. In a joyful atmosphere under beautiful vaults, you're served generous helpings of tasty dishes (especially the tripe alla fiorentina). You can eat on the terrace, too.

Duomo

Paoli
Via dei Tavolini, 12r
☎ 055 21 62 15
Closed Tue. and Aug.
Around L60,000.
If you feel like going somewhere unforgettable, this is where you should come. The vaulted room decorated with old frescoes is magnificent and the remarkable cuisine is equal to the setting.

Alfredo
Viale Don Minzoni, 3r
☎ 055 57 82 91
Closed Mon.
Around L45,000.
Here you can sample the rare tagliatelles di mare, carefully prepared by the chef Mario Tosi. The pleasant atmosphere, delightful decor and attentive service will make it a meal to remember.

Pennello
Via Dante Alighieri, 4r
☎ 055 29 48 48
Closed Sun. evening,
Mon. and Aug.
Around L40,000.
Just next to Dante's house right in the heart of the tourist district, but still sought after by Florentines, who crowd into the charming little room. The osso bucco is well worth going out of your way for.

Perseus
Viale Don Minzoni, 10r
☎ 055 58 82 26
Closed Sun. and
3 weeks in Aug.
Around L40,000.
If you want to sustain yourself with some nice grilled meat or a large mixed salad (pecorino,

Parmesan, radishes, mozzarella and prawns, for example), Giovanni Verrecchia's is the place to come. A quiet, welcoming restaurant, where the meat is cooked in front of you.

Piazza Beccaria

Le Campane
Borgo La Croce, 87r
☎ 055 23 41 101
Closed Mon.
Around L30,000.
This pizzeria just behind the little flea market doesn't look much but it has hidden delights. You'll be offered 'giant' pizzas that are as big as the table and more than enough for a meal in themselves. They're as tasty and crisp as can be, and can also be taken away.

Santa Maria Novella

I Quattro Amici
Via degli Orti Oricellari, 29
☎ 055 21 54 13
Open every day.
Around L65,000.
An excellent place to enjoy delicious fish dishes cooked with the herbs that are so frequently used in Italian cuisine. The menu tends to reflect the cuisine of the entire Mediterranean, and the Catalan-style crème brûlée (with port and caramel) is amazing. There's a remarkable choice of white wines, with live music Thursday to Saturday (Oct.-Jun). If you like good living, you'll love it here.

Croce al Trebbio
Via delle Belle Donne, 49r
☎ 055 28 70 89
Closed Mon.
Around L30,000.
A simple little trattoria serving carefully-prepared Florentine specialities. The set meals are reasonable and you can eat for as little as L21,000.

La Martinicca
Via del Sole, 27r
☎ 055 21 89 28
Closed Sun. and Aug.
Around L30,000.
Little frequented by tourists but popular with regulars, this trattoria serves fantastic cuisine that's carefully prepared and fresh. From the antipasti to the dolci, it's much appreciated by the gourmands of Florence.

Carmine

Garga
Via del Moro, 48r
☎ 055 23 98 898
Closed Mon. and
1 week around 15 Aug.
Around L70,000.
Inventive cuisine, lovingly prepared and served by the owner, who also exhibits his paintings in the restaurant. Incredible pasta and delicious baccalà al pomodor e basilico (cod in tomato and basil sauce) to savour in a warm, friendly setting.

I Raddi
Via d'Ardiglione, 47r
☎ 055 21 10 72
Closed Sun. and Aug.
Around L40,000.
A friendly, family-run restaurant serving generous helpings of Tuscan cuisine. The tris della casa (three first-rate varieties of pasta) is especially memorable. Typically Florentine.

Ponte Vecchio

Osteria del Cinghiale Bianco
Borgo San Jacopo, 43r
☎ 055 21 57 06
Closed Wed. and
3 weeks in Jul.
Around L35,000.
In this big, airy restaurant that's well known and very popular, the owner serves you homemade dishes with a smile. The L15,000 set meal is a treat.

Bordino
Via Stracciatella, 9r
☎ 055 21 30 48
Closed Sun.
Around L30,000.
A tiny trattoria in a quiet alley. The decor is plain (bare stone and old wooden tools), and the prices so reasonable that it's always full. The cuisine quite simply delicious. Try the marmitta di bolliti misti and poppa fiorentina.

Nella
Via delle Terme, 19r
☎ 055 21 89 25
Closed Sun.
Around L30,000.
Sergio Fattorini prepares typical Tuscan specialities in a simple setting. The L25,000 set meal is particularly good value.

I Tarocchi
Via dei Renai, 12n
☎ 055 23 43 912
Closed Mon.
Around L20,000.
The walls are decorated with tarot cards, but there's nothing esoteric about this restaurant. Crowded around big wooden tables you're served delicious pizza and pasta and you can end your meal with a vin santo (wine with almond-flavoured biscuits) – a feast at a remarkably low price. The restaurant is only open for dinner and has become popular, so try and avoid peak times.

Santa Croce

La Baraonda
Via Ghibellina, 67r
☎ 055 23 41 171
Closed Sun. and
Mon. lunchtime
Around L50,000.
Elena is in the kitchen and Duccio advises and serves his customers with care. It's a popular, quiet place, serving freshly-prepared Tuscan cuisine. The tagliatelles al ragù di fegatini and delicious desserts are truly memorable.

Caffè Concerto
Lungarno Colombo, 7
☎ 055 67 73 77
Closed Sun.
Around L40,000.
Gabriele Tarchiani and Marie Lorang have worked hard to build a reputation for their riverside restaurant and American stars such as Woody Allen and Tom Cruise are mad about it. The set meals change every month according to the weather and local produce and, despite the restaurant's success, the cooking remains delicious (try the maialini al latte) and the welcome is warm.

Santo Spirito

Il Cantinone
Via Santo Spirito, 6r
☎ 055 21 88 98
Closed Mon. and
2 weeks in Aug.
Around L35,000.
The menu is limited but the Tuscan cuisine is excellent (especially the fagioli all'uccelletto and the ravioli tartufati). You get a warm welcome and dine in a pretty 15th-century cellar – what more could you want?

Borgo Antico
Piazza Santo Spirito, 6r
☎ 055 21 04 37
Closed Mon.
Around L25,000.
This restaurant, in one of the city's nicest squares, is literally taken over at dinner time by a young, cosmopolitan clientele. Great pizzas and tasty meat dishes.

Tranvai
Piazza Torquato
Tasso, 14r
☎ 055 22 51 97
Closed Sun. and
15-30 Aug.
Around L25,000.
In a large, quiet square a little away from the tourist bustle, this tiny, friendly trattoria serves tasty home cooking, with a nice little house red to wash it down. Young Florentines often come here, so the restaurant soon fills up.

Ognissanti

Harry's bar
Lungarno A. Vespucci, 22r
☎ 055 23 96 700
Closed Sun and 31 Dec.
Around L70,000.
This place may have nothing in common with the famous Venetian bar of the same name, but you can enjoy a tasty sandwich or excellent steak tartare here and the Italian specialities (purea di spinacci and cotolette alla milanese) are just as good. Don't miss the apple tart – it's as light as a feather. There's even a lovely terrace overlooking the river.

À Fiesole

Carpe Diem
Via Mantellini, 2b
☎ 055 59 95 95
Closed Mon. and
1 week around 15 Aug.
Around L60,000.
A few minutes from Florence, just before you get to Fiesole, you dine in summer by candlelight on a terrace with a fabulous view of the city. The place was recently taken over and the new chef will prepare a generous helping of cozze e vongole (mussels and cockles) or a tasty bistecca alla fiorentina grigliata al pepe nero e rosmarino. All the pasta is homemade and each sort is more delicious than the last.

RESTAURANTS

WHERE TO FIND GOOD ICE CREAM

Duomo

Perchè no ?
Via dei Tavolini, 5r
☎ 055 23 98 969
Closed Tue.
A vast choice of delicious ice creams, some made from fresh fruit. Original flavours to try include mascarpone, bacio and meringa.

Il Granduca
Via dei Calzaiuoli, 57r
☎ 055 29 81 12
Closed Wed.
A great place to indulge in your favourite ice cream, that's located conveniently between the Duomo and the Piazza della Signoria. If you like ice cream, you'll love it here.

WINE BARS

Santa Croce

Fiaschetteria Vecchio Casentino
Via dei Neri, 5
Closed Mon. and Aug.
Open 5-11.30pm.
Small and friendly on the corner of two streets, this 100% Florentine establishment offers carefully-chosen menu that includes local wines and delicious cold cuts.

CAFÉ

Piazza della Signoria

Rivoire
Piazza della Signoria
Open every day.
With its great location at the foot of the old palace, Rivoire is much frequented by tourists, who come here for rest and refreshment. The prices are correspondingly high, but it's a very pleasant place to stop at dusk after a hard day of sightseeing.

PUB

Santa Maria Novella

The Fiddlers Elbow
Piazza Santa Maria Novella
Closed Wed.
Open 4.30pm-1am.
If you've a hankering after Ireland and frothy beer, this lively pub is the place for you. It has well-selected beers and tables outside in summer.

PATISSERIES

Duomo

Robiglio
Via dei Servi, 112r
☎ 055 21 27 84
Just up the road from the Duomo on the way to the Accademia, you'll come across this little patisserie selling delicious meringues and other very reasonably-priced cakes and pastries that you can enjoy with a cup of coffee.

Piazza Beccaria

Dolci e Dolcezze
Piazza C. Beccaria, 8r
☎ 055 23 45 458
Closed Mon.
Tucked away behind Santa Croce, you'll find one of the best patisseries in the city. Pick whatever takes your fancy – everything is delicious, but also relatively expensive.

CLUBS

Yab
Via de' Sassetti, 5r
(Piazza della Repubblica)
☎ 055 21 51 160
Open every day exc. Sun.
7pm-3am, closed Aug.,
entry free.
The most popular club in the city has a very varied programme of music ranging from house on Saturdays and hip-hop and rap on Mondays to 80s hits on Thursdays. If you've got something to wear, go to the fashion party on Friday – it's the day you're most likely to bump into a celebrity.

Meccanó
Viale degli Olmi
(Parco delle Cascine)
☎ 055 33 13 71
Tue.-Sat. 9pm-3am,
entry L30,000/20,000.
One of the city's fashionable spots that's frequented by young and old alike, with a variety of music ranging from piano bar to acid jazz. Look out for the Mame Prive, a disco (playing disco music) within the disco, with an open-air dance floor overlooking the Cascine park that's great in summer. If you go to the weekend theme nights, it's better to go with a regular unless you know the dress code.

Villa Kasar
Lungarno Colombo
☎ 055 67 69 12
Fri.-Sat. 9pm-3am,
closed Aug.,
entry L25,000/20,000.
Don't miss this very classy establishment, where football stars and celebrities dance side by side with young Florentine aristocrats to the sound of Latino or 80s-90s music.

Kajà
Via Pistoiese, 185
☎ 055 89 98 025
Mon., Fri. and Sat.
9.30pm-3am,
closed in summer,
entry L25,000/10,000.
Behind Cascine Station, a young, mixed crowd with a proliferation of TV and showbiz types, dance the night away to the sound of house and techno. There are DJ sessions on Mondays.

Happyland
Campi Bisenzio
Via Benedetto Croce
☎ 055 89 28 30
Open Fri., Sat.
and Sun. pm,
entry L25,000/15,000.
A pizzeria, fast-food restaurant and daytime disco with three dance floors all rolled into one, this place is frequented by a very young and trendy crowd, fond of avant-garde or commercial music. Its main advantage is an open-air swimming pool in summer.

BARS/CAFÉS

AN EVENING STROLL

If, like the Florentines, you enjoy an evening stroll, here's a route that will take about an hour and allow you to see the most important sights of the city.

Starting in the Piazza del Duomo, which will appear to you in all its glory once the hordes of tourists have left, go down the Via Roma until you come to the Piazza della Repubblica, which is filled with music coming from the Café Paszkowski on summer evenings. You may want to sit in a café terrace for a drink or ice cream as you watch the endless stream of people passing by.

Then make your way to the Piazza della Signoria via the Via Calimala and Via Porta Rossa, making a short detour on the way to see the church of Orsanmichele which is illuminated at night. After admiring the immaculate Neptune in the middle of his pool and the square mass of the Palazzo Vecchio, which is even more imposing by night than by day, cross the Uffizi courtyard, which is the favourite spot of street entertainers and tradesmen.

When you arrive at the river Arno, you'll have the best view going of the Ponte Vecchio, under its weight of little shops. Cross the bridge to reach the Oltr'Arno and the Palazzo Pitti standing alone on its stone plinth. When you come to Cosimo I's column, turn right into the Via Mazzetta, which leads to the Piazza Santo Spirito, taking care not to miss the fine view of the Via Maggio and Ponte Santa Trinità.

The Piazza Santo Spirito is a very pleasant place to eat or drink out of doors, and is the favourite haunt of young Florentines, who drink beer and chat on the church steps. A second stop at the Cabiria or Café Ricchi is a must before you make your way down the deserted Via Santo Spirito as far as the Arno at the end on the right. Here you'll see the most majestic and best-lit bridge in the city, the Ponte alla Carraia. Opposite stands the vast Palazzo Corsini, a jewel of 17th-century architecture, with its elegant balustraded terraces.

From the fan-shaped Piazza Golgoni, take the aristocratic Via dei Fossi to the Piazza Santa Maria Novella. There you'll see the church with its black and white marquetr, which appears as if it's surrounded by a halo of ethereal light. This is the second symbol of the Renaissance that placed its seal of beauty on the city. You've come full circle and can either go back to your hotel or continue the evening in the bar of your choice.

ASTROLL

More handy words and phrases

USEFUL EXPRESSIONS

I am sorry
Mi dispiace

I don't know
Non lo so

How?
Come?

Pardon me?
Prego?

Could you repeat that?
Può ripetere quello per favore?

My name is…
Mi chiamo…

A lot
Molto

Enough
Abbastanza

Nothing
Niente

AT THE HOTEL

Hotel
Albergho

Bed & breakfast/guesthouse
Pensione

I have a reservation
Ho una prenotazione

…for three people
…per tre persone

…for three nights
…per tre notti

with a double bed
con un letto matrimoniale

with twin beds
con due letti

Is breakfast included?
E compresa la prima colazione?

We are leaving tomorrow morning
Partiamo domani mattina

Suitcase
Valigia

IN THE RESTAURANT

I would like…
Vorrei…

What is the dish of the day?
Qual'è il piatto del giorno?

I would just like something to drink
Vorrei solo bere qualcosa

Wine list
Lista dei vini

Non smoking
Non Fumatori

Baked
Al forno

Grilled
Alla griglia

Poached
Cotto in bianco

Fried
Fritto

Steamed
Al vapore

MEAT AND FISH

Meat
Carne

Bacon
Pancetta

Sausage
Salsiccia

Shellfish/seafood
Molluschi/Frutta di mare

Cod
Merluzzo

Salmon
Salmone

VEGETABLES

Courgettes
Zucchini

Aubergines/eggplants
Melanzane

French beans
Fagiolini

Spinach
Spinaci

Mushrooms
Funghi

Tomato
Pomodoro

Potatoes
Patate

SUNDRIES

Crisps/peanuts
Patatine/noccioline americane

Salt/pepper
Sale/pepe

Mustard
Senape

Sugar
Zucchero

Rice
Riso

Egg
Uovo

Toast
Pane tostato

DRINKS

A glass of…
Un bicchiere di…

Tea with milk/lemon
Thè con latte/limone

Fruit juice
Succo di frutta

Hot chocolate
Cioccolata

Sparkling water
Acqua frizzante

NUMBERS

1 Uno
2 Due
3 Tre
4 Quattro
5 Cinque
6 Sei
7 Sette
8 Otto
9 Nove
10 Dieci
11 Undici
12 Dodici
13 Tredici
14 Quattordici
15 Quindici

16 Seidici	**Change money**	**Belt**
17 Diciasette	Cambiare	Cintura
18 Diciotto	**Bureau de change**	**Blouse**
19 Diciannove	Cambio	Camicetta
20 Venti	**Traveller's cheque**	**Bracelet**
	Assegno turistico	Braccialetto
TIME AND DATES	**Cash machine**	**Coat**
Morning/afternoon/	Bancomat	Cappotto
evening	**Post box**	**Dress**
La mattina/il pomeriggio/	Cassetta	Vestito
la sera	**Stamp**	**Earring**
Yesterday/today/	Francobollo	Orecchino
tomorrow	**Telephone**	**Hat**
Ieri/oggi/domani	Telefono	Capello
		Leather
DAYS OF THE WEEK	**TRAVELLING**	Cuoio
Monday	**I want to go to…**	**Jacket**
Lunedì	Voglio andare a…	Giacca
Tuesday	**Do I need to change?**	**Jeweller**
Martedì	Devo cambiare?	Gioielliere, orefice
Wednesday	**Which platform does it**	**Lingerie**
Mercoledì	**leave from?**	Biancheria intima
Thursday	Da quale binario parte?	**Purse**
Giovedì	**Bus/coach station**	Portamonete
Friday	Stazione di autobus	**Ring**
Venerdì	**Bus stop**	Anello
Saturday	Fermata d'autobus	**Scarf**
Sabato	**Airport**	Sciarpa
Sunday	Aeroporto	**Silk**
Domenica	**Taxi rank**	Seta
	Posteggio di taxi	**Socks**
IN THE TOWN	**Car**	**(or stockings)**
Can you tell me the	Macchina	Calze
way to…?	**Bicycle**	**Shirt**
Per andare a…?	Bicicletta	Camicia
What time does it	**On foot**	**Shoes**
open?	A piedi	Scarpe
A che ora apre?	**Passport**	**Skirt**
What time does it	Passaporto	Gonna
close?	**Timetable**	**Suit**
A che ora chiude?	Orario	Vestito
Here/there	**Left luggage**	**Sweater**
Qui/là	Deposito bagagli	Maglietta, golf
Near/far		**T-shirt**
Vicino/lontano	**SHOPPING**	Maglietta
Opposite	**It's too expensive**	**Trousers**
Di fronte	E troppo caro	Pantaloni
Next to	**Where can I find…?**	**Tie**
Accanto a	Dove posso trovare…?	Cravatta
On the left/on the right		**Tights**
A sinistra/a destra	**SHOPPING FOR**	Collant
Straight on	**CLOTHES AND**	**Wallet**
Sempre dritto	**ACCESSORIES**	Portafoglio
Entrance/Exit	**Bag**	
Entrata/Uscita	Borsa	